LIVING LITURGY™

FOR EXTRAORDINARY MINISTERS OF HOLY COMMUNION

Year A • 2017

Joyce Ann Zimmerman, C.PP.S.
Kathleen Harmon, S.N.D. de N.
Rev. John W. Tonkin

LITURGICAL PRESS
Collegeville, Minnesota

www.litpress.org

ISSN 1933-3129

ISBN 978-0-8146-4820-9   ISBN 978-0-8146-4845-2 (ebook)

Presented to

_____

*in grateful appreciation
for ministering as an
Extraordinary Minister
of
Holy Communion*

_____

_____

(date)

USING THIS RESOURCE

Extraordinary ministers of Holy Communion are called to serve the Christian community by ministering the Body and Blood of Christ to the Body of Christ, for by baptism we are all made members of Christ's Body. Rather than a "status symbol" in the liturgical community, these ministers are servants of the servants, as Jesus himself showed us at the Last Supper. They are called "extraordinary" not because of any personal worthiness or honor, but because the "ordinary" ministers of Holy Communion are bishops, priests, deacons, or instituted acolytes. In the typical parish situation, however, large numbers of the faithful come forward for Communion, and so in most cases lay members of the parish are designated as "extraordinary" ministers so that the Communion procession does not become disproportionately long.

Preparing for this ministry

As with all ministry, extraordinary ministers of Holy Communion must prepare themselves in order to serve their sisters and brothers in Christ well. This book is intended to be a guide and resource for that preparation. Each Sunday and some key festival days are laid out with prayer and reflections to help the Communion minister prepare each week, even when he or she is not scheduled for ministry. Some of the language of the text implies a group is present for the preparation; these texts are conveniently worded for when two or more extraordinary ministers gather for preparation, or for when these texts are shared in the context of the rite of Holy Communion with the homebound and sick.

Holy Communion for the homebound and sick

Jesus' preaching of the Good News in the Gospel is made visible by his many and varied good works on behalf of others. Perhaps more than any other group, Jesus reaches out with his healing touch to those who are sick, and this compassionate ministry continues today in the life of the church. One of the many blessings of parishes who have extraordinary ministers of Holy Communion is that those who are sick or homebound within parishes or those in hospitals and other care centers can share in the liturgical life of the parish more frequently. These ministers are reminded that the sick and suffering share in a special way in Jesus' passion. The ministers can bring hope and consolation and the strength of the Bread of Life to those who seem cut off from active participation in parish life.

Adapting this resource for Holy Communion for the homebound and sick
It is presumed that each Communion minister is familiar with the rites for Communion with the sick. There is a brief rite for those in hospitals or other care centers; this shorter rite is used when the circumstances would not permit the longer rite. The longer rite is used in ordinary circumstances and includes a Liturgy of the Word preceding the Communion rite. When using the longer rite, the opening and closing prayer given for each Sunday or festival included in this book would nicely round out the beginning and end of the service; the gospel is conveniently included to proclaim the word, and a reflection (also included for each Sunday or festival) might be shared.

Privilege and dignity
It is indeed a unique blessing to serve members of the parish as extraordinary ministers of Holy Communion, both at the parish Mass and by bringing Communion to the sick and homebound. The parish's presence through ministry to the sick and homebound is a particular sign of their dignity as members of the Body of Christ. The Communion minister is in a unique position to bring hope and comfort to those who may find little in life to comfort them. May this ministry always be a sign of Jesus' great love and compassion for all his Father's beloved children!

On the First Sunday of Advent, Jesus commands us to "stay awake" for his coming in the fullness of time. We pause at the beginning of prayer to reflect on the times when we have been so caught up in the demands of everyday living that we have not been fully awake to Jesus coming to us here and now . . .

Prayer

Eternal God, time for you is not measured by successive minutes, but by the endless love you extend to us at all times. As we await the Second Coming of your divine Son in all his glory, help us to live holy lives now and so be prepared for his many comings to us now and follow him wherever he leads us. We ask this through Christ our Lord. **Amen**.

Gospel (Matt 24:37-44)

Jesus said to his disciples: "As it was in the days of Noah, so it will be at the coming of the Son of Man. In those days before the flood, they were eating and drinking, marrying and giving in marriage, up to the day that Noah entered the ark. They did not know until the flood came and carried them all away. So will it be also at the coming of the Son of Man. Two men will be out in the field; one will be taken, and one will be left. Two women will be grinding at the mill; one will be taken, and one will be left. Therefore, stay awake! For you do not know on which day your Lord will come. Be sure of this: if the master of the house had known the hour of night when the thief was coming, he would have stayed awake and not let his house be broken into. So too, you also must be prepared, for at an hour you do not expect, the Son of Man will come."

Brief Silence

For Reflection

For us human beings, time is duration, relentless minutes ticking on. Once past, there is no recovery of lost hours. Wasted time is lost time. Wasted opportunity is lost growth. Wasted preparedness is lost encounter. There is, however, another time that cannot be measured: God's time, the fullness of time in which is the fullness of Life. God's time has no duration. This describes eternity, and even now in our measured time we experience eternity, God's time. When Jesus admonishes us to "stay awake," he is inviting attentiveness to his abiding Presence that is *now* even as its fullness is yet to come. How we live now is how we will be: taken into God's time, or left in the never ending succession of hours and days, weeks and years.

How we live in our time is a doorway into God's time. How we live in our time prepares us for Christ's Second Coming, while it also prepares us for living more fully even now. Advent calls us to immerse ourselves in God's time and to stay awake for the Life that is yet to come—and is already now.

✦ When I realize that receiving Holy Communion in the here and now is a participation in the fullness of time and Life that is to come, I . . .

Brief Silence

Prayer

Almighty and ever-living God, you offer us Life and love as we begin our Advent time of watching and waiting. May we always be attentive to your divine Presence as we beg you to draw us to love you more deeply. We ask this through Christ our Lord. **Amen**.

John the Baptist calls us in this Sunday's gospel to repent and make straight the way of the Lord. We pause at the beginning of our prayer to open ourselves to God's saving mercy . . .

Prayer

Merciful God, you sent your divine Son to call us to repentance and offer us forgiveness. May we hear his call, root out any sinfulness in our lives, and live our baptismal vows faithfully. We ask this through Christ our Lord. **Amen**.

Gospel (Matt 3:1-12)

John the Baptist appeared, preaching in the desert of Judea and saying, "Repent, for the kingdom of heaven is at hand!" It was of him that the prophet Isaiah had spoken when he said: / *A voice of one crying out in the desert, / Prepare the way of the LORD, / make straight his paths.* / John wore clothing made of camel's hair and had a leather belt around his waist. His food was locusts and wild honey. At that time Jerusalem, all Judea, and the whole region around the Jordan were going out to him and were being baptized by him in the Jordan River as they acknowledged their sins.

When he saw many of the Pharisees and Sadducees coming to his baptism, he said to them, "You brood of vipers! Who warned you to flee from the coming wrath? Produce good fruit as evidence of your repentance. And do not presume to say to yourselves, 'We have Abraham as our father.' For I tell you, God can raise up children to Abraham from these stones. Even now the ax lies at the root of the trees. Therefore every tree that does not bear good fruit will be cut down and thrown into the fire. I am baptizing you with water, for repentance, but the one who is coming after me is mightier than I. I am not worthy to carry his sandals. He will baptize you with the Holy Spirit and fire. His winnowing fan is in his hand. He will clear his threshing floor and gather his wheat into his barn, but the chaff he will burn with unquenchable fire."

Brief Silence

For Reflection

John's harsh language, unrelenting judgment, and uncompromising challenge demand a wholehearted response: Repent! Repentance is a wholly personal choice, personal act, personal demand to change. Repentance brings the favorable judgment that not only invites us to the kingdom of heaven but *is* the peace and harmony portraying the already "at hand" of God's reign. The choice to repent has consequences beyond the immediate. To repent takes us beyond John's baptism of water which brings a new human way to live. To repent is to embrace Jesus' baptism "with the Holy Spirit and fire" which brings us to a new way to live in God.

John directs to everyone his strong warning to repent. Some "acknowledged their sins," and expressed their desire to live "in the kingdom of heaven" by submitting to John's baptism with water. The "Pharisees and Sadducees" resisted repentance, claiming their descent from Abraham was enough for them to belong to "the kingdom of heaven." John's challenge to repent elicits two responses. Which response do we choose? Whether Jesus will gather us as wheat or burn us as chaff depends upon our choice.

✦ John's call to repentance reminds us that beyond receiving Holy Communion, we must . . .

Brief Silence

Prayer

Gracious God, John the Baptist challenged us to make straight our path to you. May we embrace Gospel living more faithfully and come to you with open hearts. We ask this through Christ our Lord. **Amen**.

Mary was conceived in her mother's womb without any stain of sin. In this way God prepared her to bear in her own womb "the Son of God." Let us open ourselves to God's mercy during our prayer that we too may bear God for the world . . .

Prayer

Saving God, you preserved Mary free from sin from the moment of her conception, thus preparing her to be a fitting temple for your divine Son. Have mercy on us, keep us from sin, and strengthen us to be a fitting presence of your divine Son for all those we meet. We ask this through Christ our Lord. **Amen.**

Gospel (Luke 1:26-38)

The angel Gabriel was sent from God to a town of Galilee called Nazareth, to a virgin betrothed to a man named Joseph, of the house of David, and the virgin's name was Mary. And coming to her, he said, "Hail, full of grace! The Lord is with you." But she was greatly troubled at what was said and pondered what sort of greeting this might be. Then the angel said to her, "Do not be afraid, Mary, for you have found favor with God. Behold, you will conceive in your womb and bear a son, and you shall name him Jesus. He will be great and will be called Son of the Most High, and the Lord God will give him the throne of David his father, and he will rule over the house of Jacob forever, and of his Kingdom there will be no end." But Mary said to the angel, "How can this be, since I have no relations with a man?" And the angel said to her in reply, "The Holy Spirit will come upon you, and the power of the Most High will overshadow you. Therefore the child to be born will be called holy, the Son of God. And behold, Elizabeth,

your relative, has also conceived a son in her old age, and this is
the sixth month for her who was called barren; for nothing will
be impossible for God." Mary said, "Behold, I am the handmaid of
the Lord. May it be done to me according to your word." Then the
angel departed from her.

Brief Silence

For Reflection

Mary, sinless and "full of grace" from the moment of her conception, could respond to Gabriel's words "Do not be afraid" and
embrace what God would accomplish in her. Rather than recoiling,
Mary said yes and bore "the Son of God" for the world. Despite
our own sinfulness, when we say yes, we too have nothing to fear.
If we open ourselves to God's Presence, we can also hear said to
us, "Do not be afraid." We too can say yes to God. We too can bear
God for the world.

Mary's yes choice has consequences for all of humanity:
through her the Savior of the world was born; through her divinity was wed with humanity and new Life burst forth. Simi-
larly, our own yes choices have consequences for humanity: it is
through the yes of each one of us that God chooses to make the
risen Life of the Son present in our world today. Divinity continues to be wedded to humanity through us, and for this Mary the
Mother of God is truly the model for our own daily living.

✦ "May it be done to me" is most difficult for me to say when
. . . is easiest to say when . . .

Brief Silence

Prayer

Gracious God, you call us to holiness and give us Mary as the perfect model for the way we ought to choose to live. Strengthen us
to say yes to whatever you ask of us, that one day we might join
Mary and all the saints before the throne of your holiness, offering
you praise for ever and ever. We ask this through Christ our Lord.
Amen.

In this Sunday's gospel John the Baptist sends his disciples to Jesus to ask if he is the Messiah. As we begin our prayer, let us examine our own efforts to come to know who Jesus is . . .

Prayer

Loving God, through the Word made flesh you reveal yourself to us. May we see your Presence in the persons and events of our lives and hear your word to us as it comes to us in many ways during our daily living. We ask this through Christ our Lord. **Amen**.

Gospel (Matt 11:2-11)

When John the Baptist heard in prison of the works of the Christ, he sent his disciples to Jesus with this question, "Are you the one who is to come, or should we look for another?" Jesus said to them in reply, "Go and tell John what you hear and see: the blind regain their sight, the lame walk, lepers are cleansed, the deaf hear, the dead are raised, and the poor have the good news proclaimed to them. And blessed is the one who takes no offense at me."

As they were going off, Jesus began to speak to the crowds about John, "What did you go out to the desert to see? A reed swayed by the wind? Then what did you go out to see? Someone dressed in fine clothing? Those who wear fine clothing are in royal palaces. Then why did you go out? To see a prophet? Yes, I tell you, and more than a prophet. This is the one about whom it is written: / *Behold, I am sending my messenger ahead of you; / he will prepare your way before you. /* Amen, I say to you, among those born of women there has been none greater than John the Baptist; yet the least in the kingdom of heaven is greater than he."

Brief Silence

For Reflection

Three identities are revealed in this gospel. First, John seeks to know if Jesus is "the one who is to come." Jesus does not respond with a simple yes, but invites John and his disciples to discover his identity by hearing and seeing his good works. Then Jesus reveals who John is. Even "more than a prophet," he is the messenger of the Messiah. He is the one who diverts attention from himself to prepare his hearers to accept a Messiah revealed not by power and wealth but by self-giving regard for others. Finally Jesus reveals who we are. We, "the least in the kingdom of heaven," are greater than John. How can this be?

Let us see John for who he really was—the humble messenger pointing to the Messiah. Let us see Jesus for who he really is—the Messiah-King whose power is in his being the self-giving, tender, merciful servant. Let us see ourselves for who we really are—God's beloved people who, when we minister as Jesus did, are even greater than John.

✦ When I distribute Holy Communion, I see . . . I hear . . .

Brief Silence

Prayer

Merciful God, sometimes in our pains and sorrows we are not able to see your loving Presence beckoning us to come nearer to you to find comfort and peace. As we prepare for our Christmas celebration, help us to see how you are transforming us to be the risen Presence of Christ for others. We ask this through Christ our Lord. **Amen**.

In this Sunday's gospel an angel visits Joseph in a dream and tells him not to fear taking Mary into his home as his wife. As we begin our prayer, we reflect on the times we have not allowed God to direct our own lives . . .

Prayer

God of promises, you sent your Son into our world to allay our fears and enable us to dream of one day being with you forever in the fullness of Life. As an angel assured Joseph who took Mary as his wife, assure us that we might hear your word of divine will and follow it faithfully. We ask this through Christ our Lord. **Amen**.

Gospel (Matt 1:18-24)

This is how the birth of Jesus Christ came about. When his mother Mary was betrothed to Joseph, but before they lived together, she was found with child through the Holy Spirit. Joseph her husband, since he was a righteous man, yet unwilling to expose her to shame, decided to divorce her quietly. Such was his intention when, behold, the angel of the Lord appeared to him in a dream and said, "Joseph, son of David, do not be afraid to take Mary your wife into your home. For it is through the Holy Spirit that this child has been conceived in her. She will bear a son and you are to name him Jesus, because he will save his people from their sins." All this took place to fulfill what the Lord had said through the prophet: */ Behold, the virgin shall conceive and bear a son, / and they shall name him Emmanuel, /* which means "God is with us." When Joseph awoke, he did as the angel of the Lord had commanded him and took his wife into his home.

Brief Silence

For Reflection

This story, which begins with the yes of Joseph and Mary, continues through history with our yes to opening ourselves to God's dwelling among us. The birth of this Child isn't simply a historical event that happened long ago, but is a present experience of "God is with us." Though unnamed in the gospels, we are to be the Josephs who dream dreams and the Marys who give birth to this Child who saves. "This is how the birth of Jesus Christ [comes] about": *we* say yes to God, even when we don't understand what God is asking of us. We give birth to Emmanuel in our homes, cities, nations. We are to be the risen Presence of Christ in our world, we are to make his Gospel known, and we are to do all that God commands us. This is how "God is with us." We are to give birth to Emmanuel, "God is with us." By opening ourselves to the Holy Spirit and cooperating with God's plan for our life, we, like Mary and Joseph, usher in a whole new in-breaking of God into human history. Truly, Emmanuel, "God is with us."

✦ Eucharist announces and makes present Emmanuel, "God is with us." My daily life is a living Eucharist for others when I . . .

Brief Silence

Prayer

Loving God, your Son's Body and Blood is Emmanuel, "God is with us." Awaken us to the grace of this moment, strengthen us to say yes to your holy will, and increase our eagerness for the Christmas celebration of Presence and peace. We ask this through Christ our Lord. **Amen.**

We gather in utter awe to pray and ponder so wondrous a Mystery, that the Son of God becomes one with us in the flesh. Let us raise grateful hearts to God for this gift, and open ourselves to the Mystery before us . . .

Prayer

Saving God, you sent your only-begotten Son to dwell among us. As we celebrate the mystery of Word made flesh, may we never cease to wonder at this great gift, praise you for your graciousness, and show our gratitude by the goodness of our lives. We ask this through Christ our Lord. **Amen**.

Gospel (Luke 2:1-14; from the Mass at Midnight)

In those days a decree went out from Caesar Augustus that the whole world should be enrolled. This was the first enrollment, when Quirinius was governor of Syria. So all went to be enrolled, each to his own town. And Joseph too went up from Galilee from the town of Nazareth to Judea, to the city of David that is called Bethlehem, because he was of the house and family of David, to be enrolled with Mary, his betrothed, who was with child. While they were there, the time came for her to have her child, and she gave birth to her firstborn son. She wrapped him in swaddling clothes and laid him in a manger, because there was no room for them in the inn.

Now there were shepherds in that region living in the fields and keeping the night watch over their flock. The angel of the Lord appeared to them and the glory of the Lord shone around them, and they were struck with great fear. The angel said to them, "Do not be afraid; for behold, I proclaim to you good news of great joy that will be for all the people. For today in the city of David a savior has been born for you who is Christ and Lord. And this will be a sign for you: you will find an infant wrapped in swaddling clothes and lying in a manger." And suddenly there was a multitude of the heavenly host with the angel, praising God and saying: / "Glory to God in the highest / and on earth peace to those on whom his favor rests."

Brief Silence

For Reflection

From the exalted heavenly host of angels to the lowly shepherds "living in the fields," a newness of God's Presence and glory are announced. This Good News cannot be contained in highest heavens, but must be made known to all creatures on earth. Now heaven and earth are reunited in the Mystery of perfect love. Although it is Mystery ever so rich that God should be clothed in human likeness, it is nonetheless a Mystery that touches earthy shepherds and maiden, and we ourselves as we celebrate each year the mystery of the Incarnation.

Although Joseph is not mentioned in the gospels outside of the nativity story and the finding in the temple, he is no accidental player in the Incarnation story. He is open, discerning, righteous, obedient, chaste. He models our relationship to God, to Christ, and to each other. He trusted the Mystery we celebrate. Mary gives birth to her firstborn Son. She shares him with poor shepherds. She shares him with the world. She gives over her firstborn Son and ponders the Mystery. She trusted the Mystery we celebrate. So must we.

✦ Joseph's response to the Mystery of salvation is . . . The shepherds' response is . . . Mary's response is . . . My response is . . .

Brief Silence

Prayer

O God who comes to your beloved people, you give us great joy in your enduring Presence. As we celebrate this new divine in-breaking in the Person of your Son, help us more faithfully to lead the life he came to teach us and bring us to a share in his eternal glory. We ask this through Christ our Lord. **Amen.**

As we celebrate this day in honor of the Blessed Virgin Mary, the Mother of God, let us seek God's mercy at the beginning of our prayer for the times we have been wayward children . . .

Prayer

Almighty God, you willed that the Holy Spirit overshadow Mary who gave birth to your divine Son. As we celebrate this great mystery, may we make known all that we have heard and seen. We ask this through Christ our Lord. **Amen**.

Gospel **(Luke 2:16-21)**

The shepherds went in haste to Bethlehem and found Mary and Joseph, and the infant lying in the manger. When they saw this, they made known the message that had been told them about this child. All who heard it were amazed by what had been told them by the shepherds. And Mary kept all these things, reflecting on them in her heart. Then the shepherds returned, glorifying and praising God for all they had heard and seen, just as it had been told to them.

When eight days were completed for his circumcision, he was named Jesus, the name given him by the angel before he was conceived in the womb.

Brief Silence

For Reflection

The shepherds came to the manger, encountered the newborn infant, left the stable to make "known the message," then "returned, glorifying and praising God." The passage is unclear about to where they "returned." Probably, they returned to their flocks and fields, the same shepherds yet different for all they had "heard and seen." Possibly, however, they returned to the stable seeking further affirmation for "all they had heard and seen," once again encountering this "infant lying in the manger" who surprised them, affirmed them, and called them to proclaim to all they met a most astounding message. The shepherds show us how to be affirmed in our own encounters with Jesus the Christ and how we are to reflect on this mystery of Jesus' birth and life. Before we can make "known the message," we must encounter Jesus. To affirm that it is *his* message we make known, we must keep coming back to him to encounter him anew. Mary was present when the shepherds encountered the infant in the manger. Likewise, Mary is present when we encounter her Son. She is the mother who is ever with us.

✦ Just as the shepherds "made known the message that had been told them," I make known this message by . . .

Brief Silence

Prayer

Give us strength, O saving God, to make known the message your Son came to teach us to a people who, so often, have closed their ears to hear the Good News and closed their eyes to see the wonder of his Presence. We ask this through Christ our Lord. **Amen**.

The Epiphany is the feast day celebrating the Light of Christ shining forth for all peoples to see. We pause at the beginning of our prayer to reflect on when we have failed to live in this Light . . .

Prayer

O God, at the beginning of time you created light through your mighty word. You also sent the Word to live among us to be our glorious Light. May we be his light shining for all people to see, guiding them to salvation. We ask this through Christ our Lord. **Amen**.

Gospel (Matt 2:1-12)

When Jesus was born in Bethlehem of Judea, in the days of King Herod, behold, magi from the east arrived in Jerusalem, saying, "Where is the newborn king of the Jews? We saw his star at its rising and have come to do him homage." When King Herod heard this, he was greatly troubled, and all Jerusalem with him. Assembling all the chief priests and the scribes of the people, he inquired of them where the Christ was to be born. They said to him, "In Bethlehem of Judea, for thus it has been written through the prophet: / *And you, Bethlehem, land of Judah, / are by no means least among the rulers of Judah; / since from you shall come a ruler, / who is to shepherd my people Israel."* / Then Herod called the magi secretly and ascertained from them the time of the star's appearance. He sent them to Bethlehem and said, "Go and search diligently for the child. When you have found him, bring me word, that I too may go and do him homage." After their audience with the king they set out. And behold, the star that they had seen at its rising preceded them, until it came and stopped over the place where the child was. They were overjoyed at seeing the star, and on entering the house they saw the child with Mary his mother.

They prostrated themselves and did him homage. Then they opened their treasures and offered him gifts of gold, frankincense, and myrrh. And having been warned in a dream not to return to Herod, they departed for their country by another way.

Brief Silence

For Reflection

Who is this newborn Child for whom the magi are searching, being led by a star? He is "the newborn king of the Jews." But in reality the One they seek is more: he is ruler, shepherd—the Christ. Do we ever ask, as did the magi, "Where is the newborn king of the Jews"? How diligently do we search? What star leads us? Whom do we find? How do we fit into this astounding story? How do we encounter the Light of the world?

This feast of the Epiphany celebrates the Light being manifested to all nations. This feast invites each of us to be among the seekers of the Light who do Christ homage. The Light is a welcoming, peaceful warmth to which we surrender and are overjoyed. The Light entering the darkness makes the contrast between goodness and evil that much more magnified. Those who choose to recognize the Light are drawn to give homage and open the gifts of their hearts. Those who choose darkness enter a path of trouble and destruction. What does this Light reveal in our hearts? What part of the story do we embrace?

✦ I am the Light of Christ for others when I . . .

Brief Silence

Prayer

God of light and goodness, you sent your divine Son to guide us to live in the Light of his Presence. Nourish us on our journey of overcoming darkness so we might live in the everlasting Light of your glory. We ask this through Christ our Lord. **Amen**.

In this Sunday's gospel John the Baptist announces the "Lamb of God" on whom the Spirit rests. Let us begin our prayer by reflecting on the times we have not recognized the "Lamb of God" in our midst . . .

Prayer

Almighty God, your Son is the Lamb of God who redeems us and baptizes us with the Holy Spirit. Help us to grow in knowing him, to walk more faithfully in his ways, and to reflect his glory by the goodness of our lives. We ask this through Christ our Lord. **Amen.**

Gospel (John 1:29-34)

John the Baptist saw Jesus coming toward him and said, "Behold, the Lamb of God, who takes away the sin of the world. He is the one of whom I said, 'A man is coming after me who ranks ahead of me because he existed before me.' I did not know him, but the reason why I came baptizing with water was that he might be made known to Israel." John testified further, saying, "I saw the Spirit come down like a dove from heaven and remain upon him. I did not know him, but the one who sent me to baptize with water told me, 'On whomever you see the Spirit come down and remain, he is the one who will baptize with the Holy Spirit.' Now I have seen and testified that he is the Son of God."

Brief Silence

For Reflection

John's prophetic announcement, "Behold, the Lamb of God," reveals two things about Jesus. He is "the Lamb" who will be sacrificed for the remission of "the sin of the world." He is "of God" who will "baptize with the Holy Spirit." This one, seemingly simple phrase "Lamb of God" metaphorically captures the whole saving mystery of Christ. He will be the Lamb who is sacrificed for our salvation. This "Lamb of God" will give his life so that we might have Life. This "Lamb of God" baptizes us with the Holy Spirit so that we might know him, walk in his ways, and have abundant Life.

Getting to know Jesus takes a lifetime, because knowing him is not simply an intellectual exercise, a social encounter, or a casual event. He wishes to be known so that we can grow in his holiness, in his glory, in his grace and beauty. Knowing him is more even than lifelong encounter. Knowing and being one with Jesus means sacrificing ourselves—giving ourselves over to him so that we grow more fully into the Life he offers us. Now and forever.

✦ As I come to know Jesus more deeply, what I say about him is . . .

Brief Silence

Prayer
Loving God, from of old you called prophets to call your holy people back to their covenantal relationship with you. As we encounter John the Baptist in this gospel, may we be witnesses of the Presence of the risen Christ as was John. We ask this through Christ our Lord. **Amen.**

In this gospel Jesus calls disciples to follow him. Let us pause as we begin prayer and ask God's mercy for the times we have not responded faithfully . . .

Prayer

O God, you call us to face the darkness in our lives and become the light of your divine Son shining for others. May we encounter the risen Christ, proclaim his Good News, and witness to the presence of the kingdom of heaven among us now and always. We ask this through Christ our Lord. **Amen**.

Gospel (Matt 4:12-23 [Shorter Form: Matt 4:12-17])

When Jesus heard that John had been arrested, he withdrew to Galilee. He left Nazareth and went to live in Capernaum by the sea, in the region of Zebulun and Naphtali, that what had been said through Isaiah the prophet might be fulfilled: / *Land of Zebulun and land of Naphtali, / the way to the sea, beyond the Jordan, / Galilee of the Gentiles, / the people who sit in darkness have seen a great light, / on those dwelling in a land overshadowed by death / light has arisen. /* From that time on, Jesus began to preach and say, "Repent, for the kingdom of heaven is at hand."

As he was walking by the Sea of Galilee, he saw two brothers, Simon who is called Peter, and his brother Andrew, casting a net into the sea; they were fishermen. He said to them, "Come after me, and I will make you fishers of men." At once they left their nets and followed him. He walked along from there and saw two other brothers, James, the son of Zebedee, and his brother John. They were in a boat, with their father Zebedee, mending their nets. He called them, and immediately they left their boat and their father and followed him. He went around all of Galilee, teaching in their synagogues, proclaiming the gospel of the kingdom, and curing every disease and illness among the people.

Brief Silence

For Reflection

This gospel passage tells of a turning point in Jesus' life, a turning point that lasts far longer than one day. "From that time on . . . the kingdom of heaven is at hand." "From that time on" the fulfillment of Isaiah's prophecy that "light has arisen" to dispel darkness is coming to completion. "From that time on" Jesus' public ministry is set in motion. "From that time on" disciples are called. "From that time on" encounters with Jesus lead to changed lives. Then and now. From *this* time on . . .

The kingdom of heaven is neither earthly realm nor distant place. The kingdom of heaven is present in our response to Jesus. It is our willing obedience to hear him call us, to leave everything, to follow him without counting the cost. The "kingdom of heaven is at hand" when we are hearers of Jesus' call, proclaimers of his Good News, healers of ills, guardians of God's truth, builders of virtue, fishers of people, teachers of mercy and forgiveness, prophets of new life.

✦ As I distribute Holy Communion and my face shines with the light of Christ, communicants . . .

Brief Silence

Prayer

Eternal Father, you give us all we need to become the light of Christ for others. Call us to your Presence and show us the way to the eternal light of your peace. We ask this through Christ our Lord. **Amen.**

In this gospel we hear the familiar Beatitudes. Let us seek God's mercy for the times we have not lived up to our blessedness . . .

Prayer

Holy God, you call us to empty ourselves of all that keeps us from growing in our blessedness. May we always do your holy will, grow in the Life you offer us, and rejoice in your many gifts to us. We ask this through Christ our Lord. **Amen**.

Gospel (Matt 5:1-12a)

When Jesus saw the crowds, he went up the mountain, and after he had sat down, his disciples came to him. He began to teach them, saying: / "Blessed are the poor in spirit, / for theirs is the kingdom of heaven. / Blessed are they who mourn, / for they will be comforted. / Blessed are the meek, / for they will inherit the land. / Blessed are they who hunger and thirst for righteousness, / for they will be satisfied. / Blessed are the merciful, / for they will be shown mercy. / Blessed are the clean of heart, / for they will see God. / Blessed are the peacemakers, / for they will be called children of God. / Blessed are they who are persecuted for the sake of righteousness, / for theirs is the kingdom of heaven. / Blessed are you when they insult you and persecute you and utter every kind of evil against you falsely because of me. Rejoice and be glad, for your reward will be great in heaven."

Brief Silence

For Reflection

Jesus announces the blessings for those who live in "the kingdom of heaven." In this he describes the qualities that mark true discipleship: poor in spirit, mourning loss, meek, seekers of justice, merciful, clean of heart, peacemakers, bearers of insults and persecution. To be so blessed, so happy, so fortunate requires letting go of self. All these qualities exhibit the self-emptying of Jesus himself. Blessedness is of, in, and with Jesus—and his followers. Our blessedness is both a quality of who we are and a blueprint for how we are to be and live as followers of Jesus.

Happiness is a factor of how we relate to others—we are to be Jesus' blessed Presence for others. Gospel living—taking seriously the Beatitudes—turns upside down the relationships people have with each other and invites a new world order that is the presence of God's "kingdom of heaven." And this presence of God's kingdom is not so much our own doing, as what God is accomplishing in us. Happiness—blessedness—is God's gift to those who seek God and do God's will.

✦ The letting go of self that blessedness requires includes . . .

Brief Silence

Prayer
Blessed are you, Lord God, and blessed are those who walk in the ways of the risen Christ. As you nourish us for our journey through life, help us to anticipate with joy the gift of everlasting Life you offer us. We ask this through Christ our Lord. **Amen**.

Jesus admonishes us to be salt that seasons and light that shines through our discipleship. Let us ask for his mercy and forgiveness for the times we have not been faithful disciples . . .

Prayer

Gracious God, you light our way to eternal Life as we savor the goodness you bestow upon us. Help us to encounter more deeply Jesus Christ so that we can be his light for others, leading them to a deeper union with you. We ask this through Christ our Lord. **Amen**.

Gospel (Matt 5:13-16)

Jesus said to his disciples: "You are the salt of the earth. But if salt loses its taste, with what can it be seasoned? It is no longer good for anything but to be thrown out and trampled underfoot. You are the light of the world. A city set on a mountain cannot be hidden. Nor do they light a lamp and then put it under a bushel basket; it is set on a lampstand, where it gives light to all in the house. Just so, your light must shine before others, that they may see your good deeds and glorify your heavenly Father."

Brief Silence

For Reflection

Jesus calls us to assess whether our discipleship has lost its potency because our salt has become flat and our light has become dim. The good news is that no matter how bland or dim our discipleship, Christ never throws us out, tramples us underfoot, or hides us. He calls disciples to be "the salt of the earth" and the "light of the world," yet to be such, Christ must first be *our* salt and light. We need first to encounter Christ who always remains with us, making it possible for us to mature in our discipleship.

We can be faithful disciples—salt that seasons others in Gospel living, and light that dispels the darkness of uncertainty and lack of clear direction—when we listen to Jesus and allow him to guide us. To be fruitful disciples, the first relationship we must foster is with Jesus. This relationship ensures that we are not just any salt or any light, but that of Christ. We are like salt licks attracting others to Christ; we are the light that makes clear for others the way to Christ.

✦ When I remember that I am Christ's salt and light for others, my life becomes . . .

Brief Silence

Prayer

Living and glorious God, you give us all we need to be faithful disciples of your Son, our Lord Jesus Christ. Strengthen us to be ever more faithful in our discipleship and one day be with you for ever and ever. We ask this through Christ our Lord. **Amen.**

In this gospel Jesus challenges us to enter the "kingdom of heaven" by fulfilling God's law. Let us ask for God's mercy for the times we have failed to do so . . .

Prayer

O God, you give us your law to guide us on the path of righteousness. Help us to make right choices in our daily living by ever keeping before us your law that is grounded in your goodness and truth. We ask this through Christ our Lord. **Amen**.

Gospel (Matt 5:20-22a, 27-28, 33-34a, 37
[Longer Form: Matt 5:17-37])

Jesus said to his disciples: "I tell you, unless your righteousness surpasses that of the scribes and Pharisees, you will not enter the kingdom of heaven.

"You have heard that it was said to your ancestors, *You shall not kill; and whoever kills will be liable to judgment.* But I say to you, whoever is angry with his brother will be liable to judgment.

"You have heard that it was said, *You shall not commit adultery.* But I say to you, everyone who looks at a woman with lust has already committed adultery with her in his heart.

"Again you have heard that it was said to your ancestors, *Do not take a false oath, but make good to the Lord all that you vow.* But I say to you, do not swear at all. Let your 'Yes' mean 'Yes,' and your 'No' mean 'No.' Anything more is from the evil one."

Brief Silence

For Reflection

In all the examples in this gospel that Jesus gives about the law ("You have heard"), he urges his hearers to live the law to God's intended fulfillment of it ("But I say"). The intended fulfillment of the law is the "righteousness" (right relationship with God and others) which identifies those who are the "greatest in the kingdom of heaven." *The* "greatest in the kingdom of heaven" is Jesus himself who is the fulfillment of the law in his very Person. If we are to be "greatest in the kingdom of heaven," we must encounter Jesus himself, *the* righteous One, *the* fulfillment of the law.

No law—whether divine or human—can cover all the right choices we are to make as we journey through life in community. The gospel points to what more is needed: making right choices that bring life to ourselves and others and relying on the wisdom and understanding of God who knows us better than we know ourselves. Our own choices for good—for life—can only come when we open ourselves to God's guidance and wisdom. In this is the promise of fullness of Life. In this is our life in Christ.

✦ I fulfill the law as God intended when I . . .

Brief Silence

Prayer

God of mercy and just judgment, when we keep your laws we have nothing to fear. Help us to discern what is right for our lives, to obey the spirit of your law with eagerness and joy, and one day come to share everlasting Life with you. We ask this through Christ our Lord. **Amen**.

Jesus challenges us to be perfect as our heavenly Father is perfect. As we begin our prayer, let us open ourselves to God's love and mercy . . .

Prayer

O God, holy is your name, a holiness that you share with us by giving us your divine Life. Help us to strive to treat others with the same excess of goodness and mercy that you extend to us. We ask this through Christ our Lord. **Amen.**

Gospel (Matt 5:38-48)

Jesus said to his disciples: "You have heard that it was said, *An eye for an eye and a tooth for a tooth.* But I say to you, offer no resistance to one who is evil. When someone strikes you on your right cheek, turn the other one as well. If anyone wants to go to law with you over your tunic, hand over your cloak as well. Should anyone press you into service for one mile, go for two miles. Give to the one who asks of you, and do not turn your back on one who wants to borrow.

"You have heard that it was said, *You shall love your neighbor and hate your enemy.* But I say to you, love your enemies and pray for those who persecute you, that you may be children of your heavenly Father, for he makes his sun rise on the bad and the good, and causes rain to fall on the just and the unjust. For if you love those who love you, what recompense will you have? Do not the tax collectors do the same? And if you greet your brothers only, what is unusual about that? Do not the pagans do the same? So be perfect, just as your heavenly Father is perfect."

Brief Silence

For Reflection

In our treatment of one another—even those who are our enemies—Jesus challenges us to go beyond what is expected, beyond
what we might think is reasonable or even achievable. We are to
go beyond what is human to what is divine: we are to be holy as
God is holy, to "be perfect" as God is perfect. On our own, this is
impossible! Only because of God's love for us expressed in the life
of Jesus who teaches us rightly, is this possible. Only when we
experience God's love for us first, is this possible.

Jesus commands us to keep the law in a radically different
way. We are duty-bound as "children of [the] heavenly Father"
to do more than simply what is mandated. We are to go beyond
our natural expectation about keeping laws to embrace the divine
excess with which God treats us. Acting toward others as God
acts toward us transforms us to "be perfect" as God. This radical
living of the law makes divine blessings, grace, and holiness to be
real, visible, and at hand for us.

✦ Distributing Holy Communion becomes my participation in
God's divine excess when I . . .

Brief Silence

Prayer

O God, you are holy above all others and are perfect beyond measure. As we share in the heavenly food of your Son's Body and
Blood, draw us to yourself that we might never lose sight of
the great gifts you give us. We ask this through Christ our Lord.
Amen.

Jesus tells us in this gospel that "No one can serve two masters." Let us ask for God's mercy and forgiveness for the times we have chosen to serve the wrong master . . .

Prayer

Loving God, you are a kind and merciful Master who gives us a share in your very Life. Help us to focus more single-mindedly on you, serving you as our one Master, and one day come to share the fullness of Life with you forever. We ask this through Christ our Lord. **Amen**.

Gospel (Matt 6:24-34)

Jesus said to his disciples: "No one can serve two masters. He will either hate one and love the other, or be devoted to one and despise the other. You cannot serve God and mammon.

"Therefore I tell you, do not worry about your life, what you will eat or drink, or about your body, what you will wear. Is not life more than food and the body more than clothing? Look at the birds in the sky; they do not sow or reap, they gather nothing into barns, yet your heavenly Father feeds them. Are not you more important than they? Can any of you by worrying add a single moment to your life-span? Why are you anxious about clothes? Learn from the way the wild flowers grow. They do not work or spin. But I tell you that not even Solomon in all his splendor was clothed like one of them. If God so clothes the grass of the field, which grows today and is thrown into the oven tomorrow, will he not much more provide for you, O you of little faith? So do not worry and say, 'What are we to eat?' or 'What are we to drink?' or 'What are we to wear?' All these things the pagans seek. Your heavenly Father knows that you need them all. But seek first the kingdom of God and his righteousness, and all these things will be given you besides. Do not worry about tomorrow; tomorrow will take care of itself. Sufficient for a day is its own evil."

Brief Silence

For Reflection

It is natural to worry about immediate things that affect our daily living like food and shelter, job security and paying bills. We usually don't worry about ultimate things. Our own shortsightedness can leave us quite impoverished. Jesus challenges us to a longer view: "seek first the kingdom of God and his righteousness." With this perspective our wealth is assured, but it is not a wealth counted by met needs, worry-free security, or material possessions. The wealth God offers is the Life given those embraced by God's tender love—Life lived today, tomorrow, and for eternity.

Jesus tells us that we cannot serve "two masters." Clearly, he is pitting exclusive concern ("worry") with ourselves, our wants, our needs against single-mindedly seeking "the kingdom of God and his righteousness." We are not to neglect our legitimate needs, but to keep them in proper perspective. We must "not worry" but look beyond today and even tomorrow. In everything we do, we must serve only one Master, the God who lavishly provides and cares for us—today, tomorrow, and even unto fullness of Life forever.

✦ I recognize that what I do today and even tomorrow goes beyond . . .

Brief Silence

Prayer

Loving God, you invite us to cast our worries aside and rely on your tender care and assurance. Help us to overcome useless worry about our everyday concerns, knowing that you are ever with us to guide us in right ways. We ask this through Christ our Lord. **Amen.**

As we begin our Lenten journey, let us commit ourselves to be faithful to the kind of penance that leads us to conversion of life . . .

Prayer

Merciful God, you call us to penance and conversion of life. Be with us on our Lenten journey and help us to encounter you in new ways that lead to deeper relationship with you and each other. We ask this through Christ our Lord. **Amen**.

Gospel (Matt 6:1-6, 16-18)

Jesus said to his disciples: "Take care not to perform righteous deeds in order that people may see them; otherwise, you will have no recompense from your heavenly Father. When you give alms, do not blow a trumpet before you, as the hypocrites do in the synagogues and in the streets to win the praise of others. Amen, I say to you, they have received their reward. But when you give alms, do not let your left hand know what your right is doing, so that your almsgiving may be secret. And your Father who sees in secret will repay you.

"When you pray, do not be like the hypocrites, who love to stand and pray in the synagogues and on street corners so that others may see them. Amen, I say to you, they have received their reward. But when you pray, go to your inner room, close the door, and pray to your Father in secret. And your Father who sees in secret will repay you.

"When you fast, do not look gloomy like the hypocrites. They neglect their appearance, so that they may appear to others to be fasting. Amen, I say to you, they have received their reward. But when you fast, anoint your head and wash your face, so that you may not appear to be fasting, except to your Father who is hidden. And your Father who sees what is hidden will repay you."

Brief Silence

For Reflection

Lent is the time for us to begin the process of forming a new, good habit that becomes so much a part of us that we are constantly oriented toward God and good works. Why, then, do we really perform Lenten deeds of penance (almsgiving, prayer, fasting)? Not for the passing reward of public acclaim as the gospel warns, but for the benefits of having formed new and good spiritual habits that lead us to the everlasting reward of God's grace of new Life. Our penance is thus "rewarded" by a relationship with God and each other that comes from returning to God with our whole heart.

In this Ash Wednesday gospel Jesus tells us what others ought not to see in us: penitential acts aimed at gaining adulation from others. Instead, what ought others see in us through our Lenten penance? They should see unwavering care for others through our "secret" almsgiving, prevailing love for God through our "secret" prayer, persistent self-emptying through our "secret" fasting. Lent is about developing these habits of a heart seeking conversion, these habits of a life turned toward God and others.

✦ This Lent, the penance I choose to undertake for conversion of heart is . . .

Brief Silence

Prayer

Life-giving God, you nourish us with the Body and Blood of your own Son. May we be strengthened to form the good habits of the heart which lead us to the everlasting reward of the fullness of Life. We ask this through Christ our Lord. **Amen.**

Jesus was led by the Spirit into the desert to be tempted. At the beginning of Lent and of our prayer and reflection, we pause to look within ourselves and see what tempts us and leads us away from God . . .

Prayer

Merciful God, you are ever present to us to strengthen us in face of whatever temptations we have. Help us to avoid whatever causes us to stray from your Presence, to be faithful in the Lenten penance we undertake, and to listen to your word for guidance. We ask this through Christ our Lord. **Amen**.

Gospel (Matt 4:1-11)

At that time Jesus was led by the Spirit into the desert to be tempted by the devil. He fasted for forty days and forty nights, and afterwards he was hungry. The tempter approached and said to him, "If you are the Son of God, command that these stones become loaves of bread." He said in reply, "It is written: / *One does not live on bread alone, / but on every word that comes forth / from the mouth of God.*"

Then the devil took him to the holy city, and made him stand on the parapet of the temple, and said to him, "If you are the Son of God, throw yourself down. For it is written: / *He will command his angels concerning you / and with their hands they will support you, / lest you dash your foot against a stone.*" / Jesus answered him, "Again it is written, *You shall not put the Lord, your God, to the test.*" Then the devil took him up to a very high mountain, and showed him all the kingdoms of the world in their magnificence, and he said to him, "All these I shall give to you, if you will prostrate yourself and worship me." At this, Jesus said to him, "Get away, Satan! It is written: / *The Lord, your God, shall you worship / and him alone shall you serve.*"

Then the devil left him and, behold, angels came and ministered to him.

Brief Silence

For Reflection
The Spirit led Jesus into the desert to be tempted by the devil to exercise self-serving power, to preserve his well-being, to seek worldly wealth. These temptations did not fool Jesus. Jesus knew his work was not self-promotion, but the glory of his Father and the salvation of those he came to serve. That same Spirit leads us into the desert of ourselves to encounter the demons within us, to encounter the Father's mercy and forgiveness, to encounter Jesus calling us to align our lives more closely with his. We are first grafted onto Christ at our baptism. We are plunged into the cleansing waters to be raised up to new Life. We commit ourselves to goodness and profess our relationship to God. The strength of our baptismal commitment to God must be honed in the desert of ourselves where, stripped of all that distracts us, we stand naked and hungry before Truth. Only then can we be transformed. Only then are we transformed by God into beloved daughters and sons, sisters and brothers in Christ.

✦ When I go into the desert of myself to prepare to distribute Holy Communion, my encounter with communicants becomes . . .

Brief Silence

Prayer
Gracious God, you give us the strength and nourishment to overcome any temptations. May we bring grateful hearts to worship you, knowing that you will be with us in everything we do. We ask this through Christ our Lord. **Amen.**

Peter, James, and John accompany Jesus up a mountain where they see his transfigured glory. Let us prepare ourselves to encounter the glory of Christ by calling to mind the times we have not climbed the mountain with Jesus . . .

Prayer

O God, how good it is that we reflect on the transfiguration of your Son, a foreshadowing of his risen glory! Help us to open ourselves to Christ's risen Presence and to be willing to be transformed by his word. We ask this through Christ our Lord. **Amen**.

Gospel **(Matt 17:1-9)**

Jesus took Peter, James, and John his brother, and led them up a high mountain by themselves. And he was transfigured before them; his face shone like the sun and his clothes became white as light. And behold, Moses and Elijah appeared to them, conversing with him. Then Peter said to Jesus in reply, "Lord, it is good that we are here. If you wish, I will make three tents here, one for you, one for Moses, and one for Elijah." While he was still speaking, behold, a bright cloud cast a shadow over them, then from the cloud came a voice that said, "This is my beloved Son, with whom I am well pleased; listen to him." When the disciples heard this, they fell prostrate and were very much afraid. But Jesus came and touched them, saying, "Rise, and do not be afraid." And when the disciples raised their eyes, they saw no one else but Jesus alone.

As they were coming down from the mountain, Jesus charged them, "Do not tell the vision to anyone until the Son of Man has been raised from the dead."

Brief Silence

For Reflection

"Lord, it is good that we are here." In both temptation and transfiguration we are with Jesus. The promise of the gospel—and of Jesus' life—is that resisting temptation leads us to a glory that is far greater than the false promise temptation sets before us. Resisting temptation is our journey to transfiguration, our participation in Jesus' own glory. It is our journey into the fullness of Life that conforms us more perfectly to Christ. And, Lord, how good it is that we are here!

The call of God to us is the same as that to Peter, James, and John: we must be willing to leave everything to go where God wills, to accept the self-emptying as a necessary part of being given a share in Jesus' glory, to open ourselves to Jesus' touch of word and care that transforms us into faithful disciples. We must be willing to *listen* to Jesus, learn of his ways, and embrace his paschal journey. Our journey as disciples leads us to eternal glory—foreshadowed by Jesus' transfiguration. This is worth any cost.

✦ The Eucharist manifests Christ's glory to me by . . . The way I share this glory with those I meet in my daily life is . . .

Brief Silence

Prayer

Glorious God, your Son Jesus shines bright as the sun and promises us a share in his risen glory. Help us to listen to him, follow his Gospel way of living, and one day come to share in the fullness of that glory. We ask this through Christ our Lord. **Amen.**

Jesus gives the "living water" of himself to the Samaritan woman at the well. Jesus offers us this same "living water." We pause to be mindful of whatever hinders us from drinking deeply and to ask God for pardon and mercy . . .

Prayer

God of Life, your Son is the "living water" come down from heaven to teach us to worship in "Spirit and truth." Draw us to his Presence, deepen our belief in him as the "living water," and help us to grow in our love for you, the one God whom we worship. We ask this through Christ our Lord. **Amen.**

Gospel (John 4:5-15, 19b-26, 39a, 40-42 [Longer Form: John 4:5-42])

Jesus came to a town of Samaria called Sychar, near the plot of land that Jacob had given to his son Joseph. Jacob's well was there. Jesus, tired from his journey, sat down there at the well. It was about noon.

A woman of Samaria came to draw water. Jesus said to her, "Give me a drink." His disciples had gone into the town to buy food. The Samaritan woman said to him, "How can you, a Jew, ask me, a Samaritan woman, for a drink?"—For Jews use nothing in common with Samaritans.—Jesus answered and said to her, "If you knew the gift of God and who is saying to you, 'Give me a drink,' you would have asked him and he would have given you living water." The woman said to him, "Sir, you do not even have a bucket and the cistern is deep; where then can you get this living water? Are you greater than our father Jacob, who gave us this cistern and drank from it himself with his children and his flocks?" Jesus answered and said to her, "Everyone who drinks this water will be thirsty again; but whoever drinks the water I shall give will never thirst; the water I shall give will become in him a spring of water welling up to eternal life." The woman said to him, "Sir, give me this water, so that I may not be thirsty or have to keep coming here to draw water.

"I can see that you are a prophet. Our ancestors worshiped on this mountain; but you people say that the place to worship is in Jerusalem." Jesus said to her, "Believe me, woman, the hour is coming when you will worship the Father neither on this mountain nor in Jerusalem. You people worship what you do not understand; we worship what we understand, because salvation is from the Jews. But the hour is coming, and is now here, when true worshipers will worship the Father in Spirit and truth; and indeed the Father seeks such people to worship him. God is Spirit, and those who worship him must worship in Spirit and truth." The woman said to him, "I know that the Messiah is coming, the one called the Christ; when he comes, he will tell us everything." Jesus said to her, "I am he, the one who is speaking with you."

Many of the Samaritans of that town began to believe in him. When the Samaritans came to him, they invited him to stay with them; and he stayed there two days. Many more began to believe in him because of his word, and they said to the woman, "We no longer believe because of your word; for we have heard for ourselves, and we know that this is truly the savior of the world."

Brief Silence

For Reflection

Jesus himself is the well of "living water" who draws the Samaritan woman into deeper "worship in Spirit and truth." The physical "where" of worship (Mount Gerizim for the Samaritans, the Temple Mount in Jerusalem for Jews) is far less important than that "true worshipers" do so in "Spirit and truth." The Spirit stirs the well of "living water" and reveals Jesus as truly "the one called the Christ." As the well of "living water," Jesus himself is the "where" of worship who leads us to the Father through the Spirit.

As the well of "living water," Jesus draws the townspeople into deeper belief in him as "the Christ" who "is truly the savior of the world." Believing is a matter of growing in our relationship with Jesus who is our life and salvation. His word draws us to himself and a lifelong commitment to worship in "Spirit and truth," to carry forth his saving mission, and to believe that his word is ever fruitful. Worship, mission, and believing are *the* way to "eternal life." We need only to drink of Jesus, the well of "living water."

✦ Jesus draws me to thirst for . . . He satisfies my thirst by . . .

Brief Silence

Prayer

Gracious God, you desire that we have the rich nourishment of heavenly food that only your Son can provide for us. Help us to drink deeply of his risen Life and conform ourselves more perfectly to his way of living. We ask this through Christ our Lord. **Amen**.

Jesus heals a blind beggar who comes to believe in and worship him. As we begin our time of prayer and reflection, let us ask God to remove from our hearts whatever blocks our encountering Jesus and coming to deeper faith . . .

Prayer

All-seeing God, your Presence removes our inability to see your mighty deeds of salvation. Give us insight and wisdom that we might come to deeper belief in your goodness and love, worshiping you with all our hearts. We ask this through Christ our Lord. **Amen**.

Gospel (John 9:1, 6-9, 13-17, 34-38 [Longer Form: John 9:1-41])

As Jesus passed by he saw a man blind from birth. He spat on the ground and made clay with the saliva, and smeared the clay on his eyes, and said to him, "Go wash in the Pool of Siloam"—which means Sent—. So he went and washed, and came back able to see.

His neighbors and those who had seen him earlier as a beggar said, "Isn't this the one who used to sit and beg?" Some said, "It is," but others said, "No, he just looks like him." He said, "I am."

They brought the one who was once blind to the Pharisees. Now Jesus had made clay and opened his eyes on a sabbath. So then the Pharisees also asked him how he was able to see. He said to them, "He put clay on my eyes, and I washed, and now I can see." So some of the Pharisees said, "This man is not from God, because he does not keep the sabbath." But others said, "How can a sinful man do such signs?" And there was a division among them. So they said to the blind man again, "What do you have to say about him, since he opened your eyes?" He said, "He is a prophet."

They answered and said to him, "You were born totally in sin, and are you trying to teach us?" Then they threw him out.

When Jesus heard that they had thrown him out, he found him and said, "Do you believe in the Son of Man?" He answered and said, "Who is he, sir, that I may believe in him?" Jesus said to him, "You have seen him, and the one speaking with you is he." He said, "I do believe, Lord," and he worshiped him.

Brief Silence

For Reflection

Jesus uses his own saliva to mix with the dust of the earth to bring new seeing and believing out of a blind beggar. All the man needed to do was to obey Jesus' command to "Go wash." He did so, and was recreated to see with the new eyes of faith. Through baptism we come to a new seeing and we are recreated into being more perfect members of the Body of Christ, more truth-filled images of God.

The miracle is less about a blind man receiving his sight than it is about the openness of the blind man to having an encounter with Jesus, his willingness to enter into conversation with him, and his readiness to believe and respond in worship. This gospel challenges those who are preparing for the Easter sacraments to deepen their faith in Jesus' power to recreate them as members of his Body. It challenges all of us to deepen our faith so that we, too, are recreated with ever new Life. Then, like the blind man whom Jesus helps to see, we can exclaim "I do believe" and worship with raised hearts and voices.

✦ My serving others as an extraordinary minister of Holy Communion has opened my eyes to . . .

Brief Silence

Prayer

God of Life and love, the heavenly food of your Son's Body and Blood draws us to exclaim, "I do believe!" Help our weak faith and draw us to the fullness of Life with you. We ask this through Christ our Lord. **Amen.**

Jesus raises Lazarus from the dead and reveals that he is the resurrection and the Life. Let us look into our hearts and see what choices bring us death rather than Life, and ask God for pardon and forgiveness . . .

Prayer

God of Life, your Son raised Lazarus from the dead as a sign that he has power over both death and life. During this Lent raise us from being dead to you through sin and bring us to a fuller share in your divine Life. We ask this through Christ our Lord. **Amen**.

Gospel (John 11:3-7, 17, 20-27, 33b-45
[Longer Form: John 11:1-45])

The sisters of Lazarus sent word to Jesus, saying, "Master, the one you love is ill." When Jesus heard this he said, "This illness is not to end in death, but is for the glory of God, that the Son of God may be glorified through it." Now Jesus loved Martha and her sister and Lazarus. So when he heard that he was ill, he remained for two days in the place where he was. Then after this he said to his disciples, "Let us go back to Judea."

When Jesus arrived, he found that Lazarus had already been in the tomb for four days. When Martha heard that Jesus was coming, she went to meet him; but Mary sat at home. Martha said to Jesus, "Lord, if you had been here, my brother would not have died. But even now I know that whatever you ask of God, God will give you." Jesus said to her, "Your brother will rise." Martha said, "I know he will rise, in the resurrection on the last day." Jesus told her, "I am the resurrection and the life; whoever believes in me, even if he dies, will live, and everyone who lives and believes in me will never die. Do you believe this?" She said to him, "Yes,

Lord. I have come to believe that you are the Christ, the Son of God, the one who is coming into the world."

He became perturbed and deeply troubled, and said, "Where have you laid him?" They said to him, "Sir, come and see." And Jesus wept. So the Jews said, "See how he loved him." But some of them said, "Could not the one who opened the eyes of the blind man have done something so that this man would not have died?"

So Jesus, perturbed again, came to the tomb. It was a cave, and a stone lay across it. Jesus said, "Take away the stone." Martha, the dead man's sister, said to him, "Lord, by now there will be a stench; he has been dead for four days." Jesus said to her, "Did I not tell you that if you believe you will see the glory of God?" So they took away the stone. And Jesus raised his eyes and said, "Father, I thank you for hearing me. I know that you always hear me; but because of the crowd here I have said this, that they may believe that you sent me." And when he had said this, he cried out in a loud voice, "Lazarus, come out!" The dead man came out, tied hand and foot with burial bands, and his face was wrapped in a cloth. So Jesus said to them, "Untie him and let him go."

Now many of the Jews who had come to Mary and seen what he had done began to believe in him.

Brief Silence

For Reflection

Both Martha and Mary say to Jesus, "Lord, if you had been here, / my brother would not have died." How disappointed they must have been with Jesus! Martha and Mary's expectation, hope, desire that their brother would be healed by their Friend was actually too shortsighted. Jesus intended something way beyond their experience, their imagination, their limited understanding of him and his power. Jesus intended a new revelation about himself. And a new revelation about themselves.

The raising of Lazarus has more to do with Jesus, us, and believing than it has to do with Lazarus. Jesus works an even greater miracle than healing Lazarus. By raising him from the dead he gave a clear sign that he has power over death and life.

This gospel challenges us not so much with respect to our belief in Jesus' resurrection, as in believing that our own daily dying to self is already a sign of Life we are given and a sign of the fullness of Life we will receive at our resurrection. Martha and Mary came "to believe." Have we?

✦ Coming to believe that Jesus is the resurrection and Life, I realize I am offering communicants . . .

Brief Silence

Prayer

Loving God, you bring life out of death, hope out of despair, strength out of weakness. As your Son raised Lazarus from the dead, may he bring us to new Life in you. We ask this through Christ our Lord. **Amen**.

We hear in Matthew's passion account how Jesus is betrayed, denied, abandoned. As we begin our prayer and reflection, let us ask for God's forgiveness for the times we have not been faithful to Jesus . . .

Prayer

God of joy and promise, on this day we sing hosanna to Christ our Messiah at the same time we hear of his betrayal, suffering, crucifixion, and death. Be with us through our conflicting feelings and help us see the promise of Life you give us. We ask this through Christ our Lord. **Amen**.

Gospel (Matt 27:11-54 [Longer Form: Matt 26:14–27:66])

Jesus stood before the governor, Pontius Pilate, who questioned him, "Are you the king of the Jews?" Jesus said, "You say so." And when he was accused by the chief priests and elders, he made no answer. Then Pilate said to him, "Do you not hear how many things they are testifying against you?" But he did not answer him one word, so that the governor was greatly amazed.

Now on the occasion of the feast the governor was accustomed to release to the crowd one prisoner whom they wished. And at that time they had a notorious prisoner called Barabbas. So when they had assembled, Pilate said to them, "Which one do you want me to release to you, Barabbas, or Jesus called Christ?" For he knew that it was out of envy that they had handed him over. While he was still seated on the bench, his wife sent him a message, "Have nothing to do with that righteous man. I suffered much in a dream today because of him." The chief priests and the

elders persuaded the crowds to ask for Barabbas but to destroy
Jesus. The governor said to them in reply, "Which of the two do
you want me to release to you?" They answered, "Barabbas!"
Pilate said to them, "Then what shall I do with Jesus called Christ?"
They all said, "Let him be crucified!" But he said, "Why? What
evil has he done?" They only shouted the louder, "Let him be crucified!" When Pilate saw that he was not succeeding at all, but
that a riot was breaking out instead, he took water and washed
his hands in the sight of the crowd, saying, "I am innocent of this
man's blood. Look to it yourselves." And the whole people said
in reply, "His blood be upon us and upon our children." Then he
released Barabbas to them, but after he had Jesus scourged, he
handed him over to be crucified.

Then the soldiers of the governor took Jesus inside the prae-
torium and gathered the whole cohort around him. They stripped
off his clothes and threw a scarlet military cloak about him. Weav-
ing a crown out of thorns, they placed it on his head, and a reed
in his right hand. And kneeling before him, they mocked him,
saying, "Hail, King of the Jews!" They spat upon him and took
the reed and kept striking him on the head. And when they had
mocked him, they stripped him of the cloak, dressed him in his
own clothes, and led him off to crucify him.

As they were going out, they met a Cyrenian named Simon;
this man they pressed into service to carry his cross.

And when they came to a place called Golgotha—which means
Place of the Skull—, they gave Jesus wine to drink mixed with
gall. But when he had tasted it, he refused to drink. After they had
crucified him, they divided his garments by casting lots; then they
sat down and kept watch over him there. And they placed over
his head the written charge against him: This is Jesus, the King of
the Jews. Two revolutionaries were crucified with him, one on his
right and the other on his left. Those passing by reviled him, shak-
ing their heads and saying, "You who would destroy the temple
and rebuild it in three days, save yourself, if you are the Son of
God, and come down from the cross!" Likewise the chief priests
with the scribes and elders mocked him and said, "He saved others;

he cannot save himself. So he is the king of Israel! Let him come down from the cross now, and we will believe in him. He trusted in God; let him deliver him now if he wants him. For he said, 'I am the Son of God.'" The revolutionaries who were crucified with him also kept abusing him in the same way.

From noon onward, darkness came over the whole land until three in the afternoon. And about three o'clock Jesus cried out in a loud voice, *"Eli, Eli, lema sabachthani?"* which means, "My God, my God, why have you forsaken me?" Some of the bystanders who heard it said, "This one is calling for Elijah." Immediately one of them ran to get a sponge; he soaked it in wine, and putting it on a reed, gave it to him to drink. But the rest said, "Wait, let us see if Elijah comes to save him." But Jesus cried out again in a loud voice, and gave up his spirit.

Here all kneel and pause for a short time.

And behold, the veil of the sanctuary was torn in two from top to bottom. The earth quaked, rocks were split, tombs were opened, and the bodies of many saints who had fallen asleep were raised. And coming forth from their tombs after his resurrection, they entered the holy city and appeared to many. The centurion and the men with him who were keeping watch over Jesus feared greatly when they saw the earthquake and all that was happening, and they said, "Truly, this was the Son of God!"

Brief Silence

For Reflection

It is easy to hear only the negatives in the passion accounts: Jesus is denied, betrayed, unjustly judged. He is scourged, mocked, crucified. He suffers, dies, and is buried. Yet all through the passion accounts, there are signs of life, promise, and hope. The night before he was betrayed Jesus gave his disciples a continuing memorial of his self-giving, his very Body and Blood for our nourishment as the sacrament of Life. He promised that he could rebuild the temple in three days, speaking of course about the temple of his own Body. He gave us everlasting hope that by not saving himself, he saved us.

On Palm Sunday when we sing our hosannas and bow our heads in sorrow as we hear the passion account for the first time this year, we begin the holiest week of our Christian year. It is no ordinary week, for we celebrate Jesus' unreserved self-giving. Holy Week brings before us the demands of self-giving. All of our daily living throughout the year reminds us that, ultimately, like Jesus we must give ourselves over to God so that God might give us divine Life.

✦ This Holy Week, what I can do to prepare myself for Easter Sunday are . . .

Brief Silence

Prayer

Life-giving God, you allowed your Son to die on the cross so that we might learn that death is not all there is. Draw us to your Son's risen Presence that we might always seek the salvation and fullness of Life you offer us. We ask this through Christ our Lord. **Amen**.

On Holy Thursday we celebrate Jesus' great love—so great that he sat at table even with the one who would betray him. As we begin our prayer and reflection, we pause to open our hearts to the healing which Jesus brings through his love and forgiveness . . .

Prayer

God of gifts and surprises, receiving your Son's Body and Blood never ceases to amaze us, to encourage us, to draw us to your love. We raise our hearts in gratitude to you for this great gift of the Eucharist. Help us always to receive it with gratitude, awe, and reverence. We ask this through Christ our Lord. **Amen.**

Gospel (John 13:1-15)

Before the feast of Passover, Jesus knew that his hour had come to pass from this world to the Father. He loved his own in the world and he loved them to the end. The devil had already induced Judas, son of Simon the Iscariot, to hand him over. So, during supper, fully aware that the Father had put everything into his power and that he had come from God and was returning to God, he rose from supper and took off his outer garments. He took a towel and tied it around his waist. Then he poured water into a basin and began to wash the disciples' feet and dry them with the towel around his waist. He came to Simon Peter, who said to him, "Master, are you going to wash my feet?" Jesus answered and said to him, "What I am doing, you do not understand now, but you will understand later." Peter said to him, "You will never wash my feet." Jesus answered him, "Unless I wash you, you will have no inheritance with me." Simon Peter said to him, "Master, then not only my feet, but my hands and head as well." Jesus said to him, "Whoever has bathed has no need except to have his feet washed, for he is clean all over; so you are clean, but not all." For he knew who would betray him; for this reason, he said, "Not all of you are clean."

So when he had washed their feet and put his garments back on and reclined at table again, he said to them, "Do you realize what I have done for you? You call me 'teacher' and 'master,' and rightly so, for indeed I am. If I, therefore, the master and teacher, have washed your feet, you ought to wash one another's feet. I have given you a model to follow, so that as I have done for you, you should also do."

Brief Silence

For Reflection

Jesus giving us his Body and Blood and his giving us a model for loving service are two faces of the same coin; they both are actions that draw us to focus on the good of the other in self-giving. We are able to love those who wrong us, betray us, deny us because Jesus has given us the example: "he loved them to the end." We prove our love by doing likewise. Although most of Jesus' beloved disciples "betrayed" him, he still "loved them to the end." We are able to love those who wrong us because Jesus has already reconciled us to God and each other by giving himself in self-sacrifice. We prove our love by doing likewise and serving others, even those who wrong us—to the end.

Jesus is not naive—he tells of betrayal and of everyone among the disciples not being clean. But these human weaknesses do not hold him back from drawing everyone to his love feast. Jesus desires to love us and draws our love out of us. Let the love feast begin. Now and always.

✦ Jesus' self-giving love moves me to . . . Even when I am weak, his love heals me to . . .

Brief Silence

Prayer

O God, the perfect love between you and your divine Son is the model of how we are to love one another. Through your self-giving love, show us how to serve you in one another. We ask this through Christ our Lord. **Amen.**

57

Easter fills us with joy for our Lord is risen! As we prepare to pray and ponder this great mystery, let us reflect on why we believe and how we might come to stronger belief . . .

Prayer

God of joy, you raised your Son to new Life and in that resurrection recreate all of us in this same Life. Be with us as we celebrate this great mystery, increase our joy and belief, and bring us one day to share in the fullness of risen Life. We ask this through Christ our Lord. **Amen.**

Gospel (John 20:1-9 [or Matt 28:1-10 or Luke 24:13-35])

On the first day of the week, Mary of Magdala came to the tomb early in the morning, while it was still dark, and saw the stone removed from the tomb. So she ran and went to Simon Peter and to the other disciple whom Jesus loved, and told them, "They have taken the Lord from the tomb, and we don't know where they put him." So Peter and the other disciple went out and came to the tomb. They both ran, but the other disciple ran faster than Peter and arrived at the tomb first; he bent down and saw the burial cloths there, but did not go in. When Simon Peter arrived after him, he went into the tomb and saw the burial cloths there, and the cloth that had covered his head, not with the burial cloths but rolled up in a separate place. Then the other disciple also went in, the one who had arrived at the tomb first, and he saw and believed. For they did not yet understand the Scripture that he had to rise from the dead.

Brief Silence

For Reflection

Here is the mystery of Easter: we want to see and believe, but since resurrection is so out of our human experience we simply can't understand. Belief came gradually to those first witnesses, and then only when they had a personal encounter with Jesus (some disciples ate and drank with him at Emmaus). Our own belief in the risen Jesus gradually grows throughout our life as we continually encounter him in our own eating and drinking with him. We encounter the risen Jesus in Eucharist when we eat and drink *with him*—when Jesus' very Body and Blood become our nourishment. We also encounter the risen Jesus in each other when we witness by the goodness of our lives to Gospel values. We encounter the risen Jesus in the sure joy that comes from reconciled relationships with each other that witness to our reconciled relationship with God. This is the Easter mystery: "he had to rise from the dead." He *had* to so that in the Easter mystery darkness becomes light, death becomes life, sacrifice becomes love, grief becomes joy, unbelief becomes belief.

✦ Those who help me to see and believe in the risen Jesus are . . . because . . .

Brief Silence

Prayer

Glorious God of the resurrection, you draw us into this great mystery by our sharing in the Body and Blood of your divine Son. May our joy be complete and our strength the very Life you have given us. We ask this through Christ our Lord. **Amen.**

Easter is a season that reminds us of our baptism and that brings us to celebrate the risen Christ among us. We pause now to ready ourselves to pray and ponder these Easter mysteries . . .

Prayer

God of joy, you draw us to believe in the resurrection by your Presence and love. Increase our belief and be with us as we celebrate this great mystery of Life coming from death. We ask this through Christ our Lord. **Amen**.

Gospel (John 20:19-31)

On the evening of that first day of the week, when the doors were locked, where the disciples were, for fear of the Jews, Jesus came and stood in their midst and said to them, "Peace be with you." When he had said this, he showed them his hands and his side. The disciples rejoiced when they saw the Lord. Jesus said to them again, "Peace be with you. As the Father has sent me, so I send you." And when he had said this, he breathed on them and said to them, "Receive the Holy Spirit. Whose sins you forgive are forgiven them, and whose sins you retain are retained."

Thomas, called Didymus, one of the Twelve, was not with them when Jesus came. So the other disciples said to him, "We have seen the Lord." But he said to them, "Unless I see the mark of the nails in his hands and put my finger into the nailmarks and put my hand into his side, I will not believe."

Now a week later his disciples were again inside and Thomas was with them. Jesus came, although the doors were locked, and stood in their midst and said, "Peace be with you." Then he said to Thomas, "Put your finger here and see my hands, and bring your hand and put it into my side, and do not be unbelieving, but believe." Thomas answered and said to him, "My Lord and my God!" Jesus said to him, "Have you come to believe because you have seen me? Blessed are those who have not seen and have believed."

Now, Jesus did many other signs in the presence of his disciples that are not written in this book. But these are written that you may come to believe that Jesus is the Christ, the Son of God, and that through this belief you may have life in his name.

Brief Silence

For Reflection

The absent Thomas could not bring himself to believe that Jesus was alive, for he had not yet encountered the risen Jesus. Thomas insists on seeing and touching Jesus before he can believe that he is truly alive and well. A week later, confronted by the risen Jesus, Thomas's obstinate doubt becomes unwavering belief: "My Lord and my God!" Both the disciples and Thomas's shifts in who and how they were had everlasting effects on them. In fact, from this gospel we can tease out myriad shifts: mourning to joy, fear to peace, sinfulness to forgiveness, being behind locked doors to being sent out, inertia to empowerment by the Holy Spirit, not seeing to seeing, obstinate disbelief to acclamation of faith, life before Jesus' resurrection to new "life in his name." For those who believe, Jesus' resurrection shifts their self-understanding and their purpose in life, enabling them to see all things as new. The struggle to believe is no less than the struggle to recognize and encounter the risen Jesus. Do we believe?

✦ The manner of my distributing Holy Communion helps communicants see, touch, and believe in the risen Jesus when I . . .

Brief Silence

Prayer

Gracious God, your Son gives us his risen Body and Blood as our nourishment and strength. May it bring us to deeper belief in the Easter mystery and to one day share the fullness of risen Life. We ask this through Christ our Lord. **Amen**.

Let us prepare ourselves through our prayer and reflection to encounter the risen Jesus in the Scriptures and the breaking of the bread . . .

Prayer

Almighty God, you are ever present to us in word and sacrament. Strengthen us not only to hear your word, but also to live it. Nourish us to be the Body of Christ for others. We ask this through Christ our Lord. **Amen**.

Gospel (Luke 24:13-35)

That very day, the first day of the week, two of Jesus' disciples were going to a village seven miles from Jerusalem called Emmaus, and they were conversing about all the things that had occurred. And it happened that while they were conversing and debating, Jesus himself drew near and walked with them, but their eyes were prevented from recognizing him. He asked them, "What are you discussing as you walk along?" They stopped, looking downcast. One of them, named Cleopas, said to him in reply, "Are you the only visitor to Jerusalem who does not know of the things that have taken place there in these days?" And he replied to them, "What sort of things?" They said to him, "The things that happened to Jesus the Nazarene, who was a prophet mighty in deed and word before God and all the people, how our chief priests and rulers both handed him over to a sentence of death and crucified him. But we were hoping that he would be the one to redeem Israel; and besides all this, it is now the third day since this took place. Some women from our group, however, have astounded us: they were at the tomb early in the morning and did not find his body; they came back and reported that they had indeed seen a vision of angels who announced that he was alive. Then some of those with us went to the tomb and found things just as the women had described, but him they did not see." And he said to them, "Oh, how foolish you are! How slow of heart to believe all that the prophets spoke! Was it not necessary that the Christ should suffer these things and enter into his glory?" Then beginning with Moses and all the prophets, he interpreted to them what referred to him in all the Scriptures. As they approached the village to which they were going, he gave the impression that he was going on farther. But they urged him, "Stay with us, for it is nearly evening and the day is almost over." So he went in to stay with them. And it happened that, while he was with them at table, he took bread, said the blessing, broke it, and gave it to them. With that their eyes were opened and they recognized him, but he vanished from their sight. Then they said to each other, "Were not our hearts burning within us while he spoke to us on the way and opened the Scriptures to us?" So they set out at once and returned to Jerusalem where they found gathered together the eleven and those with them who were saying, "The Lord has truly been raised and has appeared to Simon!" Then the two recounted what had taken place on the way and how he was made known to them in the breaking of the bread.

Brief Silence

For Reflection

The two disciples on the road to Emmaus had given up on "Jesus the Nazarene" as the "one to redeem Israel." They did not persevere in looking for Jesus, although they "were [still] conversing about all the things that had occurred." They hadn't quite given up, but their hope was not strong enough to bring them to stay in Jerusalem to determine if Jesus truly "was alive."

The two disciples allowed their perseverance to waver; belief in a dead-but-now-alive Jesus was beyond their experience, beyond their capacity. But the risen Jesus searched them out, walked with them, broke bread with them. Their encounter led to an overwhelming transformation moving them from unbelief to belief. Further, after returning to Jerusalem, their newfound belief was confirmed by a community who attested that "The Lord has truly been raised." We must choose this same journey today, over and over again: encounter the risen Jesus, come to deeper belief, witness to others his risen Presence. Our perseverance in proclaiming Easter joy must grow as our belief in the risen One grows. It takes a lifetime of doing to learn that perseverance pays off.

✦ The opening of the Scriptures prepares me to encounter the risen Jesus in the breaking of the bread when . . .

Brief Silence

Prayer

Redeeming God, how easy it is to miss the Presence of the risen Christ! May your grace help us see him in the people we meet each day and the events that shape our lives. We ask this through Christ our Lord. **Amen**.

At our baptism we first became members of the Good Shepherd's flock. Let us prepare ourselves to hear his voice and during our prayer and reflection listen with open hearts . . .

Prayer
Shepherd God, you never let us stray far from your loving embrace. Help us to hear your Son's voice, follow him more faithfully, and stay close to him and the risen Life he offers us. We ask this through Christ our Lord. **Amen**.

Gospel (John 10:1-10)
Jesus said: "Amen, amen, I say to you, whoever does not enter a sheepfold through the gate but climbs over elsewhere is a thief and a robber. But whoever enters through the gate is the shepherd of the sheep. The gatekeeper opens it for him, and the sheep hear his voice, as the shepherd calls his own sheep by name and leads them out. When he has driven out all his own, he walks ahead of them, and the sheep follow him, because they recognize his voice. But they will not follow a stranger; they will run away from him, because they do not recognize the voice of strangers." Although Jesus used this figure of speech, the Pharisees did not realize what he was trying to tell them.

So Jesus said again, "Amen, amen, I say to you, I am the gate for the sheep. All who came before me are thieves and robbers, but the sheep did not listen to them. I am the gate. Whoever enters through me will be saved, and will come in and go out and find pasture. A thief comes only to steal and slaughter and destroy; I came so that they might have life and have it more abundantly."

Brief Silence

For Reflection

There is only one true Shepherd. This "shepherd calls his own sheep by name and leads them out"—nay, he *drives* them out. Moreover, the shepherd "walks ahead" of the sheep, leading and guiding them. Thus, we have a two-way relationship with our Shepherd. On the one hand, he drives us out of our comfort zone to risk being his disciples. When we are reluctant to go, he gives us a push, sometimes prodding us to go even where we do not wish. Taking up our Shepherd's mission can be as dangerous for us as it was for him. On the other hand, the Shepherd goes before us with guidance and care. Even when we face danger—face ridicule, rejection, denial—he is there to protect us. We know our true Shepherd from strangers or "thieves and robbers" by the sound of his voice calling each of us by name. Yes, he calls each of us by name. Each of us is important. Each of us has a name. Do we hear him calling us by name? Are we willing to be driven by him? to be led by him?

✦ As I speak "Body [Blood] of Christ" to communicants, I am the voice of the Good Shepherd calling them to abundant Life when I . . .

Brief Silence

Prayer

O good God, your risen Son, our Good Shepherd, guides us and protects us without fail. Help us to be open to wherever he leads us, knowing that we journey toward the fullness of his risen Life and glory. We ask this through Christ our Lord. **Amen.**

At our baptism we were united with the risen Christ who is our way and truth and life. Let us surrender ourselves to God so that we may be faithful followers of Jesus . . .

Prayer

God our Father, your Son Jesus said to the disciples that he is the way and the truth and the life. Fill us with that truth and life, that we might be faithful followers of his way. We ask this through Christ our Lord. **Amen**.

Gospel (John 14:1-12)

Jesus said to his disciples: "Do not let your hearts be troubled. You have faith in God; have faith also in me. In my Father's house there are many dwelling places. If there were not, would I have told you that I am going to prepare a place for you? And if I go and prepare a place for you, I will come back again and take you to myself, so that where I am you also may be. Where I am going you know the way." Thomas said to him, "Master, we do not know where you are going; how can we know the way?" Jesus said to him, "I am the way and the truth and the life. No one comes to the Father except through me. If you know me, then you will also know my Father. From now on you do know him and have seen him." Philip said to him, "Master, show us the Father, and that will be enough for us." Jesus said to him, "Have I been with you for so long a time and you still do not know me, Philip? Whoever has seen me has seen the Father. How can you say, 'Show us the Father'? Do you not believe that I am in the Father and the Father is in me? The words that I speak to you I do not speak on my own.

The Father who dwells in me is doing his works. Believe me that I am in the Father and the Father is in me, or else, believe because of the works themselves. Amen, amen, I say to you, whoever believes in me will do the works that I do, and will do greater ones than these, because I am going to the Father."

Brief Silence

For Reflection

The ongoing struggle to believe more deeply is the ongoing struggle to come to know Jesus and become more like him. This risen Jesus is not elusive; he is encountered in the "ministry of the word," in the breaking of bread, in taking care of the needs of others, in allowing God to act in us to build us into the Body of Christ, in our announcing God's praises. The real challenge of this gospel, then, is to expand our seeing and believing to recognize the many, varied, and surprising ways Jesus comes to us. And to become for others those ways.

Jesus says to Thomas, "I am the way and the truth and the life." Jesus is the way: he is the path to the Father. Jesus is the truth: he is the revelation of who God is. Jesus is the life: he is risen Life for all those who believe in him. Believing is "be-living"—surrendering ourselves to him in all we are and in all we do. Through him and with him and in him *we* become "the way and the truth and the life."

✦ Holy Communion makes visible Jesus as the way and the truth and the life in that . . .

Brief Silence

Prayer

Eternal Father, your house has many dwelling places, and you call us to be at home with you. Grant that we may be worthy of the indwelling of your Holy Spirit and find our way to an eternal home with you. We ask this through Christ our Lord. **Amen.**

Jesus calls us to keep his commandments and he promises the gift of his Spirit who strengthens us to respond faithfully. As we begin our prayer and reflection, may we open ourselves to his Spirit who dwells within us . . .

Prayer

Gracious God, you send your Spirit of truth and life to dwell within us and show us the way of Gospel living. May our way of relating to others show them the love you have for us. We ask this through Christ our Lord. **Amen**.

Gospel (John 14:15-21)

Jesus said to his disciples: "If you love me, you will keep my commandments. And I will ask the Father, and he will give you another Advocate to be with you always, the Spirit of truth, whom the world cannot accept, because it neither sees nor knows him. But you know him, because he remains with you, and will be in you. I will not leave you orphans; I will come to you. In a little while the world will no longer see me, but you will see me, because I live and you will live. On that day you will realize that I am in my Father and you are in me and I in you. Whoever has my commandments and observes them is the one who loves me. And whoever loves me will be loved by my Father, and I will love him and reveal myself to him."

Brief Silence

For Reflection

Loving Jesus as he asks requires us to *believe* and *live* in such a way that others *know* the resurrection is real, that Jesus is really present, that Jesus still cares for us deeply. Our love for Jesus is shown in the same way as the early disciples showed their love—by practical doing in our everyday living. We are to proclaim the living Christ by the way we heal hurts in others; bring a caring touch to those who are ailing in any way; strengthen those who are weak or paralyzed by fear, doubt, or selfishness; encourage those weighed down with too much stress, work, or indecision. Jesus even sends us the help we need to love, believe, and live in this way.

Jesus' commandments entail much more than doing this or avoiding that. His commandments are to love as he loved, believe as he believed, live as he lived. His commandments are the most self-engaging and challenging of all! How comforting, then, when Jesus says "I will not leave you orphans." No, we are not orphans: the risen Jesus comes to us. How? In "the Spirit of truth."

◆ The manner of my distributing Holy Communion is a proclamation of Jesus' love for each communicant when I . . .

Brief Silence

Prayer

Loving God, your commandments are not a burden and they guide us in right ways. As we grow in our love for you and each other, may we be ever more faithful to whatever you ask of us. We ask this through Christ our Lord. **Amen.**

Jesus commissioned us to carry forth his saving mission. May our prayer and reflection strengthen us to continue this awesome ministry . . .

Prayer

Faithful God, you are ever present to us, never leaving us alone as we struggle to be faithful to the mission your Son Jesus entrusted to us. May we be open to the Spirit who teaches us all things and guides us in the way of righteousness. We ask this through Christ our Lord. **Amen.**

Gospel (Matt 28:16-20)

The eleven disciples went to Galilee, to the mountain to which Jesus had ordered them. When they saw him, they worshiped, but they doubted. Then Jesus approached and said to them, "All power in heaven and on earth has been given to me. Go, therefore, and make disciples of all nations, baptizing them in the name of the Father, and of the Son, and of the Holy Spirit, teaching them to observe all that I have commanded you. And behold, I am with you always, until the end of the age."

Brief Silence

For Reflection

Jesus ordered his disciples to a mountain, a place in Scripture of divine encounter and divine revelation. The encounter: Jesus promises to be with them "until the end of the age." His Presence is his farewell gift to the disciples. The revelation: they are to take up his saving mission by making "disciples of all nations" through baptizing and teaching. The disciples are his farewell gift to the world. Taking up his saving mission, so are we.

It takes us a lifetime of following Jesus and proclaiming his Good News to learn how gifted we are and what a gift we are to others. What the disciples hadn't yet come fully to believe was that Jesus would always remain with them, giving them strength. Through the Spirit. There was a startling newness to what Jesus was doing and the message he was conveying. Never before had someone been present among them who entrusted them to such a saving mission. Never before had someone so completely shared power. Never before had someone promised the most potent power—the Holy Spirit who is with us "until the end of the age."

✦ Jesus' promise "I am with you always" encourages me to . . .

Brief Silence

Prayer

Holy God, Jesus ascended into the heavens to take his place at your right hand. May we spread his Good News throughout the world, being his risen Presence for all we meet. We ask this through Christ our Lord. **Amen.**

Let us prepare ourselves for fruitful prayer and reflection by opening ourselves to God's glorious Presence . . .

Prayer

God of glory, you call us to the same self-giving that Jesus continues to show us. Draw us to yourself and help us to be faithful to Gospel living, witnessing to your glory in all we do. We ask this through Christ our Lord. **Amen.**

Gospel (John 17:1-11a)

Jesus raised his eyes to heaven and said, "Father, the hour has come. Give glory to your son, so that your son may glorify you, just as you gave him authority over all people, so that your son may give eternal life to all you gave him. Now this is eternal life, that they should know you, the only true God, and the one whom you sent, Jesus Christ. I glorified you on earth by accomplishing the work that you gave me to do. Now glorify me, Father, with you, with the glory that I had with you before the world began.

"I revealed your name to those whom you gave me out of the world. They belonged to you, and you gave them to me, and they have kept your word. Now they know that everything you gave me is from you, because the words you gave to me I have given to them, and they accepted them and truly understood that I came from you, and they have believed that you sent me. I pray for them. I do not pray for the world but for the ones you have given me, because they are yours, and everything of mine is yours and everything of yours is mine, and I have been glorified in them.

And now I will no longer be in the world, but they are in the world, while I am coming to you."

Brief Silence

For Reflection

The disciples, so often the beneficiaries of Jesus' instruction, are now the beneficiaries of Jesus' prayer for them. But his instruction and his prayer are part of his overall work that reaches a climax when he is glorified at the hour of his death and resurrection. We who belong to the family of Jesus continue his work and share in his glory as we share in his death and resurrection. We can never separate resurrection from suffering—interpreted as dying to self for the good of others. Taking up Jesus' mission means self-giving. No wonder Jesus prays for his disciples!

The gospel is ultimately about the mutual giving between Jesus and the Father, and our being called into the same Life of mutual self-giving, and into their Life of glory. We are to give ourselves to God and one another in love and service. In this is God's glory and ours. God is glorified by Jesus' work of salvation. Jesus is glorified by those who hear and accept his words, believe in him, and continue his saving mission. By our glorifying Jesus, God glorifies us and gives us "eternal life."

✦ In my daily living, I share Jesus' self-gift to others when I . . .

Brief Silence

Prayer

Glorious God of the resurrection, your Son's death and resurrection bring you glory. Help us faithfully to die to ourselves and rise to new Life in the risen Christ, bringing you glory by the lives we live. We ask this through Christ our Lord. **Amen.**

At our baptism we first received the gift of the Holy Spirit. Let us prepare to pray and ponder the divine Presence within us and among us . . .

Prayer

Creating God, you breathe life into all of your beloved people. May we be respectful of this life, preserve it at all costs, and one day come to eternal Life with you. We ask this through Christ our Lord. **Amen.**

Gospel (John 20:19-23)

On the evening of that first day of the week, when the doors were locked, where the disciples were, for fear of the Jews, Jesus came and stood in their midst and said to them, "Peace be with you." When he had said this, he showed them his hands and his side. The disciples rejoiced when they saw the Lord. Jesus said to them again, "Peace be with you. As the Father has sent me, so I send you." And when he had said this, he breathed on them and said to them, "Receive the Holy Spirit. Whose sins you forgive are forgiven them, and whose sins you retain are retained."

Brief Silence

For Reflection

In John's gospel Pentecost takes place on Easter evening. The giving of new Life on Easter and the giving of the Spirit on Pentecost coalesce in the one Body of Christ, the church. Something entirely new has happened. This Body is filled with the joy of divine Presence, the grace of risen peace, the eagerness of being sent forth, the breath of new creation, the power of forgiveness. Each day when we—Christ's Body, the church—allow the Holy Spirit to work in and through us, Easter-Pentecost happens anew. Each day when we open ourselves to the breath-life of the Holy Spirit, we ourselves are made anew. There is no end to the new Life that the risen Jesus and his Spirit breathe into us. Breath means life. Breath is precious. Breath enables us to be. In this gospel Jesus breathes new Life into his disciples. This breath-life is the Holy Spirit, a divine Person who recreates us into someone entirely new. There is no end to our re-creation in the Spirit, in the Body of Christ.

✦ Jesus breathes the Spirit into me and . . .

Brief Silence

Prayer

God of peace and love, your Spirit empowers us to forgive and heal, to preach and teach, to love and be loved. Help us, the Body of Christ, to surrender ourselves to the newness of Life you bring us. We ask this through Christ our Lord. **Amen.**

We honor during our prayer and reflection the Most Holy Trinity, the community of divine Persons who loves and saves us. Let us open ourselves to such a gracious God . . .

Prayer

O triune God, you are worthy of all praise and exaltation. Increase our love for you, that we might give your triune Majesty glory in all we do. We ask this through Christ our Lord. **Amen**.

Gospel (John 3:16-18)

God so loved the world that he gave his only Son, so that everyone who believes in him might not perish but might have eternal life. For God did not send his Son into the world to condemn the world, but that the world might be saved through him. Whoever believes in him will not be condemned, but whoever does not believe has already been condemned, because he has not believed in the name of the only Son of God.

Brief Silence

For Reflection

The Holy Trinity desires that we humans participate in their inner Life. We are destined to be with God now and forever. God chose to create and redeem humanity in an unequaled act of love. This gospel reminds us that God is gracious, sharing divine Life with us: "God so loved" us that God "gave his only Son" so that "the world might be saved." Yes, God sent the Son so that we might have Life. Divine Life and love extend beyond the inner intimacy of the three Persons of the Holy Trinity to us in an eternal, shared love drawing us toward a fuller share in God. This is salvation: a share in God, in God's Life.

The mystery of the Trinity calls us to go both beyond ourselves and deeper into ourselves—to an intimacy with God that delights us and brings us to share that delight with others. Thus is the trinitarian grace, love, and fellowship manifested in our midst. God is triune mystery, yes! But even more mystery-laden is that God shares divine Self with us in such a gracious manner and "receives us" as God's very own.

✦ I experience God as a loving trinity of Persons when . . .

Brief Silence

Prayer

Eternal, triune God, your love for us is immeasurable and the Life you give us surpasses anything we could desire. Help us to live faithfully the Good News your Son teaches us and one day come to share the fullness of Life with you for all eternity. We ask this through Christ our Lord. **Amen.**

We celebrate the mystery of Jesus' gift of himself to us—his very Body and Blood given for our eternal Life. As we begin our time of prayer and reflection, let us ponder what keeps us from allowing this Gift to transform our lives . . .

Prayer

Nourishing God, Jesus Christ gives us his Body and Blood for our salvation. May we grow in our self-understanding as his Body given for the life of the world. We ask this through Christ our Lord. **Amen**.

Gospel (John 6:51-58)

Jesus said to the Jewish crowds: "I am the living bread that came down from heaven; whoever eats this bread will live forever; and the bread that I will give is my flesh for the life of the world."

The Jews quarreled among themselves, saying, "How can this man give us his flesh to eat?" Jesus said to them, "Amen, amen, I say to you, unless you eat the flesh of the Son of Man and drink his blood, you do not have life within you. Whoever eats my flesh and drinks my blood has eternal life, and I will raise him on the last day. For my flesh is true food, and my blood is true drink. Whoever eats my flesh and drinks my blood remains in me and I in him. Just as the living Father sent me and I have life because of the Father, so also the one who feeds on me will have life because of me. This is the bread that came down from heaven. Unlike your ancestors who ate and still died, whoever eats this bread will live forever."

Brief Silence

For Reflection

In this gospel Jesus *is* the bread that is the *living* bread; this is *all* we need to "live forever." The reasoning is simple enough: by partaking of Jesus' Body and Blood we *become* what we eat—we become one Body in which we all share. This is the "Holy Communion" that assures us of who we are as baptized Christians—the Body of Christ. This is why Eucharist is (and remains throughout our life) a sacrament of *initiation*: we are constantly being fed on the Bread of Life and are constantly drawn more deeply into being who we are—members of the one Body of Christ. As members of Christ's Body, we are to be his life poured out in our everyday Gospel living.

Heaven is above. Forever is beyond. Life is fleeting. But Life eternal is here and now in Jesus, "the living bread" who "came down from heaven" to give himself "for the life of the world." We who eat his flesh and drink his blood have eternal Life *now*. Heaven is not above. Forever is not beyond. Life is not fleeting. Because Jesus is *living* bread.

✦ My ministry helps me become more perfectly "living bread" for others whenever I . . .

Brief Silence

Prayer

Bounteous God, you nourish us with the Bread of Life and the wine of salvation. Help us to become more perfectly "living bread" for others and one day share with you the fullness of Life. We ask this through Christ our Lord. **Amen.**

Jesus tells us that in God's eyes we are worth more than many sparrows. As we begin our prayer and reflection, let us reflect on the times we have not acted according to the worth God bestows on us . . .

Prayer

God of hope and protection, you are ever near us keeping us from whatever can destroy us. Help us to be open to your Presence, listen to your guidance, and live the Gospel fearlessly. We ask this through Christ our Lord. **Amen**.

Gospel (Matt 10:26-33)

Jesus said to the Twelve: "Fear no one. Nothing is concealed that will not be revealed, nor secret that will not be known. What I say to you in the darkness, speak in the light; what you hear whispered, proclaim on the housetops. And do not be afraid of those who kill the body but cannot kill the soul; rather, be afraid of the one who can destroy both soul and body in Gehenna. Are not two sparrows sold for a small coin? Yet not one of them falls to the ground without your Father's knowledge. Even all the hairs of your head are counted. So do not be afraid; you are worth more than many sparrows. Everyone who acknowledges me before others I will acknowledge before my heavenly Father. But whoever denies me before others, I will deny before my heavenly Father."

Brief Silence

For Reflection

In this gospel Jesus talks about fear: whom and what we should fear and whom and what we need not fear. Jesus begins with the bold statement, "Fear no one." Yet, in the next breath he tells us to "be afraid of the one who can destroy / both soul and body." Does Jesus contradict himself? No, not really. He is helping us sort out fear. We need not fear when we choose to live and "speak in the light" and acknowledge Jesus as Lord. Proclaiming the gospel can bring frightening results, for sure. People may misunderstand us, scorn us, turn on us. Certainly this happened to Jesus. We can overcome this fear, however. We know that when we align ourselves with Jesus and "proclaim on the housetops" what he has revealed to us, we are not alone. Our greatest source of audacity—of proclaiming Jesus' Good News and acting boldly—is the assurance that God has every hair on our head counted. God counts us worthy to be disciples of the divine Son, and even if others try to "kill the body," God will protect and bring to everlasting Life those who are faithful.

◆ I am fearless about being a follower of Jesus when . . .

Brief Silence

Prayer

O God, you grant us great dignity and worth and never lose sight of our presence. Strengthen us to proclaim boldly and fiercely Jesus' Good News from the housetops, from sea to sea, from day to day all our lives. We ask this through Christ our Lord. **Amen.**

Jesus urges us to put him above everyone and everything—even family. As we begin our prayer and reflection, we ask his mercy for the times we have not kept him as the center of our lives . . .

Prayer

Almighty God, we depend on you for everything, even our very lives. Help us to show our gratitude for your many gifts by striving with ever greater fervor to keep your divine Son at the center of our lives. We ask this through Christ our Lord. **Amen**.

Gospel (Matt 10:37-42)

Jesus said to his apostles: "Whoever loves father or mother more than me is not worthy of me, and whoever loves son or daughter more than me is not worthy of me; and whoever does not take up his cross and follow after me is not worthy of me. Whoever finds his life will lose it, and whoever loses his life for my sake will find it. Whoever receives you receives me, and whoever receives me receives the one who sent me. Whoever receives a prophet because he is a prophet will receive a prophet's reward, and whoever receives a righteous man because he is a righteous man will receive a righteous man's reward. And whoever gives only a cup of cold water to one of these little ones to drink because the little one is a disciple— amen, I say to you, he will surely not lose his reward."

Brief Silence

For Reflection

It is pretty difficult for us to be single-minded about anything! In this Sunday's gospel Jesus is calling his apostles (and us) to single-mindedness. Jesus clearly states that he is to be above everyone and everything in our lives—even family. This is a pretty radical single-mindedness! But this does not mean that we ignore others. Jesus also says that whoever receives his followers receives him. Jesus is reminding us that our relationship to him is expressed in our relationship with each other. In giving and receiving we make evident that Jesus is the center and focus of our lives. In giving and receiving we lose our lives for the sake of others. In giving and receiving we find fullness of Life—Jesus himself.

We can't receive unless someone gives. When we think about it, so much of our lives depends upon the generosity of others. And all life and everything we do depends upon the utter generosity of God. God gives everything. God's greatest Gift, of course, is the divine Son. Jesus Christ is to be the center of our lives.

✦ My manner of distributing Holy Communion indicates that Jesus is the center and focus of my life when I . . .

Brief Silence

Prayer

God of heaven and earth, you nourish us with the gift of your divine Son's very Body and Blood. Strengthen us to live as he did, to love as he did, to keep you at the center of our lives as he did. We ask this through Christ our Lord. **Amen**.

Jesus invites us to come to him because his yoke is easy and his burden is light. We pause now to ask for mercy for the times we have failed to come to him . . .

Prayer

Father, Lord of heaven and earth, you are revealed to us through the Presence and saving mission of your divine Son. Give us rest when we pause during our busy day with its burdens to be attentive to your Presence and love. We ask this through Christ our Lord. **Amen**.

Gospel (Matt 11:25-30)

At that time Jesus exclaimed: "I give praise to you, Father, Lord of heaven and earth, for although you have hidden these things from the wise and the learned you have revealed them to little ones. Yes, Father, such has been your gracious will. All things have been handed over to me by my Father. No one knows the Son except the Father, and no one knows the Father except the Son and anyone to whom the Son wishes to reveal him.

"Come to me, all you who labor and are burdened, and I will give you rest. Take my yoke upon you and learn from me, for I am meek and humble of heart; and you will find rest for yourselves. For my yoke is easy, and my burden light."

Brief Silence

For Reflection

What is our greatest labor and burden? Getting to know the Father through the Son. On our own, we labor under a chafing and unwieldy yoke. However, when we come to Jesus, he shoulders our labor by teaching us, revealing his Father to us, and sharing our burden. How do we come to Jesus? By being filled with the same meekness and humility of heart he has, emptying ourselves of ourselves to be filled with him. Then our yoke becomes easy and our burden light.

Heavy burdens—either in daily life or in discipleship—are not what God desires for us. God's will is that we recognize divine Presence coming to us in the person of Jesus. He comes to place on our shoulders not life's burdens which we ourselves make, but his own yoke of knowledge which is not a weight or shackle but a freeing relationship of love and care. Being yoked to Jesus involves a process of deepening relationship with him that leads to a deepening relationship with his Father. Knowing Jesus is knowing the Father.

✦ When I consider that my greatest labor and burden is getting to know the Father through the Son, I . . .

Brief Silence

Prayer

Gracious God, you ease our burdens and nourish us on our journey toward everlasting happiness with you. May we ease the burdens of others, bringing to all we meet rest and comfort. We ask this through Christ our Lord. **Amen.**

God sows the seed of the divine Word so that salvation can spread to the ends of the earth. As we settle into our prayer and reflection, let us look into our hearts to see where we have failed to hear and understand God's word . . .

Prayer

Mighty God, you spoke and all that is came to be. Your greatest word to us is in your divine Son, the Word made flesh. Open our hearts to hear him and then produce abundant fruit by living as he did. We ask this through Christ our Lord. **Amen**.

Gospel (Matt 13:1-9 [Longer Form: Matt 13:1-23])

On that day, Jesus went out of the house and sat down by the sea. Such large crowds gathered around him that he got into a boat and sat down, and the whole crowd stood along the shore. And he spoke to them at length in parables, saying: "A sower went out to sow. And as he sowed, some seed fell on the path, and birds came and ate it up. Some fell on rocky ground, where it had little soil. It sprang up at once because the soil was not deep, and when the sun rose it was scorched, and it withered for lack of roots. Some seed fell among thorns, and the thorns grew up and choked it. But some seed fell on rich soil and produced fruit, a hundred or sixty or thirtyfold. Whoever has ears ought to hear."

Brief Silence

For Reflection

Jesus tells a parable about sowing the seed-word, receptivity to the seed-word, and fruitfulness of the seed-word. Ultimately, to bear fruit the seed-word must take root in rich soil. And we can take the parable and its interpretation one step further. The sower and seed is Jesus himself, *the* Word. The rich soil is our own hearts open to hearing and understanding that Word. Because Jesus' word challenges us to conform ourselves more perfectly to him, we tend to close our hearts to his voice. Are our hearts open?

"Such large crowds gathered around" Jesus. He is scattering "the word of the kingdom" far and wide. Yet, many "look but do not see and hear but do not listen or understand." These look for the wrong seed and its fruit. Jesus is the Sower who is sowing the seed of himself, *the* Word of God. Leave the sowing of the seed to God—God does so with abandon and produces abundance. Leave the listening with our hearts to each of us—which we must also do with abandon to produce abundance.

✦ My manner of distributing Holy Communion indicates that God's word has taken root in me in that . . .

Brief Silence

Prayer

God of abundance and blessings, you nourish us with the seed of your word and the Bread of Life. May we bear fruit with these great gifts you have given us. We ask this through Christ our Lord. **Amen**.

The "kingdom of heaven" is like wheat that grows among weeds, a small seed that becomes a large bush, yeast that leavens a large batch. Let us ask for God's mercy for the times we have not opened ourselves to the presence of the "kingdom of heaven" . . .

Prayer

O God, you are ever patient with us as we work to harvest the good seed of your word among us. Help us to speak your word well and be patient as you when we serve others. We ask this through Christ our Lord. **Amen**.

Gospel (Matt 13:24-30 [Longer Form: Matt 13:24-43])

Jesus proposed another parable to the crowds, saying: "The kingdom of heaven may be likened to a man who sowed good seed in his field. While everyone was asleep his enemy came and sowed weeds all through the wheat, and then went off. When the crop grew and bore fruit, the weeds appeared as well. The slaves of the householder came to him and said, 'Master, did you not sow good seed in your field? Where have the weeds come from?' He answered, 'An enemy has done this.' His slaves said to him, 'Do you want us to go and pull them up?' He replied, 'No, if you pull up the weeds you might uproot the wheat along with them. Let them grow together until harvest; then at harvest time I will say to the harvesters, "First collect the weeds and tie them in bundles for burning; but gather the wheat into my barn."'"

Brief Silence

For Reflection

"The kingdom of heaven is like . . ." Whatever parable Jesus uses to teach about the kingdom of heaven, always at issue is growth, abundance, increase. While "the enemy" may try to thwart the kingdom, in the end God will prevail. So, "the kingdom of heaven is like" those of us who hear and live the Good News Jesus teaches. We ourselves are "the kingdom of heaven" when we live according to God's ways, accepting the gracious will of God as the rule of our lives.

Jesus describes the kingdom of heaven as we presently experience it with room for growth and maturation: there are weeds among the wheat, a bush is in growth, the dough is rising. In this present age we are to live with patience and confident assurance that the kingdom of heaven will become fully manifest in us: we will be a harvest, we will be a large bush, we will be a loaf of bread. The mystery of the kingdom, of course, is that while the end is guaranteed—life will come forth—all of us must live faithfully and work diligently if we wish to reap the fruits of following God's will—Life everlasting.

✦ For me, the "kingdom of heaven" is like . . . because . . .

Brief Silence

Prayer

O God, you do not sow weeds among us, but the good fruit of your love and care. Sow in us the seed of your goodness and patience, that one day we might enjoy the harvest of the fullness of Life with you. We ask this through Christ our Lord. **Amen.**

Jesus teaches us about the incomparable Treasure that is given to those who choose to live in the "kingdom of heaven." Let us ask for God's mercy for the times we have chosen not to live in God's kingdom . . .

Prayer

O God, your kingdom is not a realm of this world, but is made visible in our seeking to do your holy will. Help us to be faithful in living the Gospel, for this is your will for us. We ask this through Christ our Lord. **Amen.**

Gospel (Matt 13:44-52 or Matt 13:44-46)

Jesus said to his disciples: "The kingdom of heaven is like a treasure buried in a field, which a person finds and hides again, and out of joy goes and sells all that he has and buys that field. Again, the kingdom of heaven is like a merchant searching for fine pearls. When he finds a pearl of great price, he goes and sells all that he has and buys it. Again, the kingdom of heaven is like a net thrown into the sea, which collects fish of every kind. When it is full they haul it ashore and sit down to put what is good into buckets. What is bad they throw away. Thus it will be at the end of the age. The angels will go out and separate the wicked from the righteous and throw them into the fiery furnace, where there will be wailing and grinding of teeth.

"Do you understand all these things?" They answered, "Yes." And he replied, "Then every scribe who has been instructed in the kingdom of heaven is like the head of a household who brings from his storeroom both the new and the old."

Brief Silence

For Reflection

What "the kingdom of heaven is like" is not just a treasure, pearl, or fish net, not some inanimate object located in some physical place, even if these would enhance our net worth greatly. In all three of these gospel metaphors, the persons mentioned are committing themselves to an action-response. The "kingdom of heaven" is present in searching for, sacrificing for, and sorting for our greatest Treasure—God's very Life. We must "sell" all that we are—empty ourselves—so the Life God gives us freely and lavishly is ours forever.

The "kingdom of heaven" is visible in our seeking God above everyone and everything else. The treasure we go out to seek isn't some *thing* in some *place*; it is nothing less than the very *Presence and Life of God* that is breaking in upon us now but which is only fully realized in the future. Now here is where the surprise of the gospel comes in: the kingdom of heaven isn't some object or realm that we can identify *physically*; instead it is the gift of divine Presence and Life God gives us.

✦ When I reflect on my choices and actions in daily living, I learn my treasure is . . .

Brief Silence

Prayer

O holy God, you offer us your Life and holiness as signs of the presence of the kingdom of heaven. Strengthen us to seek your Presence and live according to your will. We ask this through Christ our Lord. **Amen**.

Peter, James, and John see the glory of God in the transfigured Jesus. As we begin our prayer and reflection, let us reflect on the times we have not opened ourselves to Jesus' Presence and seen his risen glory . . .

Prayer

Glorious God, you transfigured your Son before Peter, James, and John and gave them a glimpse of the glory that awaits us all. Grant us the grace to open our eyes and see the Presence of the risen Jesus in all his glory in the people and events of our everyday lives. We ask this through Christ our Lord. **Amen**.

Gospel (Matt 17:1-9)

Jesus took Peter, James, and his brother, John, and led them up a high mountain by themselves. And he was transfigured before them; his face shone like the sun and his clothes became white as light. And behold, Moses and Elijah appeared to them, conversing with him. Then Peter said to Jesus in reply, "Lord, it is good that we are here. If you wish, I will make three tents here, one for you, one for Moses, and one for Elijah." While he was still speaking, behold, a bright cloud cast a shadow over them, then from the cloud came a voice that said, "This is my beloved Son, with whom I am well pleased; listen to him." When the disciples heard this, they fell prostrate and were very much afraid. But Jesus came and touched them, saying, "Rise, and do not be afraid." And when the disciples raised their eyes, they saw no one else but Jesus alone. As they were coming down from the mountain, Jesus charged them, "Do not tell the vision to anyone until the Son of Man has been raised from the dead."

Brief Silence

For Reflection

Moses and Elijah represent the law and prophecy of the old covenant. But with Jesus' transfiguration, we see the promise of change, of something entirely new taking place. When the voice from the cloud tells the three apostles to "listen to" Jesus, they will hear something new, they will be challenged to embrace something new, they will be called to participate in a mystery only now being revealed in its fullness.

Peter wants to pitch tents and stay in the brightness and promise. But this cannot be. They must come "down from the mountain" and travel with Jesus to Jerusalem, through their denials and doubts, through their dying to their old lives and selves, through the "old" into the "new." Only then can they grasp the extent to which God desires to possess us, to draw us into divine Life, to nurture us into the new covenant, the new relationship, God wishes to have with us through the divine Son. Jesus' new covenant promises us a share in his risen Life. In the transfiguration of Jesus, Peter, James, and John see their own glorification. And so do we.

✦ What helps me see in the face of each communicant the face of the transfigured Jesus is . . .

Brief Silence

Prayer

Eternal God, your glory shines throughout the universe in the brightness of your Presence. You nourish us on your Son's Body and Blood in preparation for our own participation in your glory for all eternity. We ask this through Christ our Lord. **Amen**.

Jesus commands Peter to come to him on the stormy sea. Let us prepare ourselves to come to Jesus on the stormy seas of our own faith journey . . .

Prayer

Almighty God, your Son Jesus called to Peter to come to him across the stormy sea. When we face the inevitable storms of our daily living, help us to remember that Jesus is there, waiting for us to come to him to bring us to safety and peace. We ask this through Christ our Lord. **Amen.**

Gospel (Matt 14:22-33)

After he had fed the people, Jesus made the disciples get into a boat and precede him to the other side, while he dismissed the crowds. After doing so, he went up on the mountain by himself to pray. When it was evening he was there alone. Meanwhile the boat, already a few miles offshore, was being tossed about by the waves, for the wind was against it. During the fourth watch of the night, he came toward them walking on the sea. When the disciples saw him walking on the sea they were terrified. "It is a ghost," they said, and they cried out in fear. At once Jesus spoke to them, "Take courage, it is I; do not be afraid." Peter said to him in reply, "Lord, if it is you, command me to come to you on the water." He said, "Come." Peter got out of the boat and began to walk on the water toward Jesus. But when he saw how strong the wind was he became frightened; and, beginning to sink, he cried out, "Lord, save me!" Immediately Jesus stretched out his hand and caught Peter, and said to him, "O you of little faith, why did you doubt?" After they got into the boat, the wind died down. Those who were in the boat did him homage, saying, "Truly, you are the Son of God."

Brief Silence

For Reflection

Peter brazenly tests Jesus about his identity: "Lord, if it is you
. . . " It is that same Peter who becomes frightened and cries
out to be saved when he does what Jesus commands him to do:
"Come." With challenging truthfulness and saving power, Jesus
responds both to Peter's brazenness and to his fright. When we
act like Peter, Jesus responds to us as he did to Peter. We must
not forget that Jesus unfailingly expends his power to bring us
to salvation.

Only Jesus can remove the stumbling blocks that keep us from
recognizing him, from coming to him when he calls us, and from
losing our courage. Here is why Peter's challenge to Jesus is so
exposing: Jesus' identity is assured (he saved Peter); Peter's (our)
trust in Jesus' power is still weak, still needs to be strengthened
(Peter "became frightened"). The good news of this gospel is that
challenge doesn't lead to "drowning," but to a revelation of who
Jesus is. Challenge leads to putting ourselves into the hands of the
only One who is unfailingly trustworthy, the only One who can
truly save, the only One who calls us to become someone more
than we already are.

✦ I hesitate to come to Jesus when . . . I most quickly respond
when Jesus commands me to "Come!" when . . .

Brief Silence

Prayer

O God, you show us in many ways your great power and your
desire that we be saved. Through the nourishment of the Eucharist strengthen us to trust more deeply in your protection and care
and one day share in the eternal safety of your everlasting Life.
We ask this through Christ our Lord. **Amen**.

We celebrate Mary, who was always faithful to the prompting of the Holy Spirit and was lifted up body and soul into heaven. Let us reflect on how faithful we have been to the prompting of the Holy Spirit in our lives . . .

Prayer

Heavenly Father, you assumed Mary, the mother of your divine Son, body and soul into heaven. As Mary was faithful to the mission you gave her to bear your Son for the world, help us to witness to your Son's Presence among us and be faithful as Mary. We ask this through Christ our Lord. **Amen.**

Gospel (Luke 1:39-56)

Mary set out and traveled to the hill country in haste to a town of Judah, where she entered the house of Zechariah and greeted Elizabeth. When Elizabeth heard Mary's greeting, the infant leaped in her womb, and Elizabeth, filled with the Holy Spirit, cried out in a loud voice and said, "Blessed are you among women, and blessed is the fruit of your womb. And how does this happen to me, that the mother of my Lord should come to me? For at the moment the sound of your greeting reached my ears, the infant in my womb leaped for joy. Blessed are you who believed that what was spoken to you by the Lord would be fulfilled."

And Mary said: / "My soul proclaims the greatness of the Lord; / my spirit rejoices in God my Savior / for he has looked with favor upon his lowly servant. / From this day all generations will call me blessed: / the Almighty has done great things for me, / and holy is his Name. / He has mercy on those who fear him / in every generation. / He has shown the strength of his arm, / and has scattered the proud in their conceit. / He has cast down the mighty from their thrones, / and has lifted up the lowly. / He has filled the hungry with good things, / and the rich he has sent away empty. / He has come to the help of his servant Israel / for he has remembered his promise of mercy, / the promise he made to our fathers, / to Abraham and his children forever."

Mary remained with her about three months and then returned to her home.

Brief Silence

For Reflection

After traveling "to the hill country in haste," Mary "entered the house of Zechariah." No doubt not merely a dwelling, a "house," but a "home" where she and Elizabeth lovingly encountered not only each other, but the infants in their wombs joyfully encountered each other as well. The Holy Spirit is at work in this gospel as well as in the whole mystery of the Incarnation. The Holy Spirit makes each of us into a "home."

The Holy Spirit overshadowed Mary, filling her with "the fruit of [her] womb." The Holy Spirit filled Elizabeth, inspiring her to recognize Mary as the "mother of my Lord." The Holy Spirit remained with Mary throughout her life, empowering her spirit to rejoice in God her Savior. Because of Mary's faithful response to the prompting of the Holy Spirit, she was lifted body and soul into heaven, her true home. Like Mary, all we are and are able to do as faithful disciples of the beloved Son is prompted by the Holy Spirit. Because of our faithful response, we too will be lifted up. Our true home is where our heart is to be—with God.

✦ I experience being lifted up by God when . . . to . . . for . . .

Brief Silence

Prayer

Gracious God, you come to make your home with us through the indwelling of the Holy Spirit and through our eating and drinking the Body and Blood of your risen Son. Keep us faithful to your Presence and never let us stray from you. We ask this through Christ our Lord. **Amen.**

God's healing mercy is unbounded— even to Jesus reaching out to the bold and persistent Canaanite woman who asks for her daughter to be healed in this gospel. Let us recall God's healing mercy to us . . .

Prayer

Welcoming God, your Son came to extend salvation to all peoples. Grant us the persistence of the woman in the gospel when we come to Jesus for help, that one day we might be fully healed of all that alienates us from you and enjoy the fullness of Life with you forever. We ask this through Christ our Lord. **Amen**.

Gospel **(Matt 15:21-28)**

At that time, Jesus withdrew to the region of Tyre and Sidon. And behold, a Canaanite woman of that district came and called out, "Have pity on me, Lord, Son of David! My daughter is tormented by a demon." But Jesus did not say a word in answer to her. Jesus' disciples came and asked him, "Send her away, for she keeps calling out after us." He said in reply, "I was sent only to the lost sheep of the house of Israel." But the woman came and did Jesus homage, saying, "Lord, help me." He said in reply, "It is not right to take the food of the children and throw it to the dogs." She said, "Please, Lord, for even the dogs eat the scraps that fall from the table of their masters." Then Jesus said to her in reply, "O woman, great is your faith! Let it be done for you as you wish." And the woman's daughter was healed from that hour.

Brief Silence

For Reflection

The Canaanite woman demonstrates the kind of faith needed to
be healed by Jesus and to receive God's gift of salvation, the kind
of faith that brings us into divine embrace. Her faith was visible
in three habits of the heart: awareness that she needed Jesus' healing intervention, persistence against all odds, and concern not
only for herself but for her daughter. Her great faith moved Jesus
to have "pity on" her. Anyone who approaches God with this kind
of great faith will be given healing and salvation. We too must
develop and grow in the habits of the heart that make visible the
great faith necessary for our healing and salvation.

Here is the twist of this gospel: a seemingly unwelcome situation gives way to one in which everyone is welcome. Jesus initially
declares that his mission is only to "the house of Israel," and, con-
sequently, harshly rebuffs the Canaanite woman. Then a change
occurs. The encounter between Jesus and the woman reveals the
unrestricted welcome of Jesus, the power of great faith, and the
universality of salvation for those who believe.

✦ What I could learn from the Canaanite woman when I am
faced with resistance or rebuff is . . .

Brief Silence

Prayer

Faithful God, increase our faith, deepen our love for you, and help
us to trust in your care and mercy. Through the Eucharist we
receive, help us to develop habits of the heart that make room for
all we encounter. We ask this through Christ our Lord. **Amen**.

Peter acknowledges that Jesus is "the Christ, the Son of the living God." Let us open our hearts to encounter this same Christ who is present among us, his church gathered in his name . . .

Prayer

O God of the old and the new, you raised up prophets to guide your people back to faithfulness to the covenant. Open us to Jesus who offers us a new covenantal relationship with you and help us to grow in our understanding of who he is for us. We ask this through Christ our Lord. **Amen**.

Gospel (Matt 16:13-20)

Jesus went into the region of Caesarea Philippi and he asked his disciples, "Who do people say that the Son of Man is?" They replied, "Some say John the Baptist, others Elijah, still others Jeremiah or one of the prophets." He said to them, "But who do you say that I am?" Simon Peter said in reply, "You are the Christ, the Son of the living God." Jesus said to him in reply, "Blessed are you, Simon son of Jonah. For flesh and blood has not revealed this to you, but my heavenly Father. And so I say to you, you are Peter, and upon this rock I will build my church, and the gates of the netherworld shall not prevail against it. I will give you the keys to the kingdom of heaven. Whatever you bind on earth shall be bound in heaven; and whatever you loose on earth shall be loosed in heaven." Then he strictly ordered his disciples to tell no one that he was the Christ.

Brief Silence

For Reflection

Throughout their history prophets had guided the Jewish people in the ways of God. Prophets had called them back to covenantal fidelity. Prophets had warned the Jewish people about impending punishment when they strayed from God through being stiff-necked, self-reliant, and unfaithful. The disciples could not be prepared for who Jesus is—the new Adam, the new Moses. They could not be prepared for the wholly new covenant Jesus was offering through who he was. They could not be prepared for the new church, the new beloved people they themselves would become.

Indeed, Jesus is a prophet, but so much more: he is "the Christ, the Son of the living God." Nothing short of a revelation by the "heavenly Father" could make this known to Peter. Nothing short of a revelation by the community of believers who acknowledge Jesus as "the Christ" and remain ever faithful to his saving mission could continue to make this known even to our day. The church is a fluidity of persons cemented together by the common bond of faithfully living the mystery of who Christ is. And who we are in him.

✦ I would answer Jesus' question about his identity by saying he is . . .

Brief Silence

Prayer

Saving God, you revealed to Peter that Jesus is the Messiah, your very Son. You reveal him to us as our Savior each time we receive his Body and Blood in Holy Communion. Help us to be faithful to his Presence. We ask this through Christ our Lord. **Amen**.

Jesus tells the disciples that he must suffer and be killed before he will be raised up. As followers of Jesus, we can expect no less in our own lives. We ask God for the strength to be faithful . . .

Prayer

Sometimes, dear Lord, the message of the Gospel is so difficult for us to hear. We don't like to hear the call to die to self for the good of others. Yet, that is how we enter into the fullness of Life with you. Strengthen us to give ourselves over to you and others. We ask this through Christ our Lord. **Amen**.

Gospel (Matt 16:21-27)

Jesus began to show his disciples that he must go to Jerusalem and suffer greatly from the elders, the chief priests, and the scribes, and be killed and on the third day be raised. Then Peter took Jesus aside and began to rebuke him, "God forbid, Lord! No such thing shall ever happen to you." He turned and said to Peter, "Get behind me, Satan! You are an obstacle to me. You are thinking not as God does, but as human beings do."

Then Jesus said to his disciples, "Whoever wishes to come after me must deny himself, take up his cross, and follow me. For whoever wishes to save his life will lose it, but whoever loses his life for my sake will find it. What profit would there be for one to gain the whole world and forfeit his life? Or what can one give in exchange for his life? For the Son of Man will come with his angels in his Father's glory, and then he will repay all according to his conduct."

Brief Silence

For Reflection

Who wouldn't recoil, like Peter, when Jesus says that he would "suffer greatly . . . and be killed," especially when he says that this is also the lot of those who faithfully follow him. Jesus' curt command to Peter—"Get behind me, Satan!"—points to the crux of the challenge: we are to think like God, not like humans. In God's saving plan, we must lose our life for Jesus' sake—only in this way can we share in Jesus' risen Life. No human instinctively understands or naively embraces this. God's love alone reveals this mystery and strengthens us as we surrender ourselves to it.

We always need to hear Jesus' *whole* message about the paschal mystery: we must lose our life in order to find it. The suffering and death *always* lead to new Life. We know this because Jesus has already shown us the way. His prophecy about his passion and death *includes* his announcement of being raised to new Life. The good news-bad news question really is a non-question for Jesus' disciples. Whatever suffering and death we embrace, we know includes a share in Jesus' risen Life.

✦ I've experienced life coming from "death" when . . .

Brief Silence

Prayer

Saving God, redemption was gained for us by the obedience of your Son, even to the point of suffering and dying on the cross. Help us to embrace whatever suffering comes our way, uniting it with that of your Son, and become more like him in our self-giving. We ask this through Christ our Lord. **Amen.**

We come together to pray in Jesus' name. Let us pause to look within ourselves to see if we are doing anything that disrupts our unity as the community of Jesus' followers . . .

Prayer

Merciful God, you give us all good things and call us to be in union with you and each other. Forgive us for the times we have strayed from right relationship with you and each other, and bring us to the peace of reconciliation. We ask this through Christ our Lord. **Amen**.

Gospel (Matt 18:15-20)

Jesus said to his disciples: "If your brother sins against you, go and tell him his fault between you and him alone. If he listens to you, you have won over your brother. If he does not listen, take one or two others along with you, so that 'every fact may be established on the testimony of two or three witnesses.' If he refuses to listen to them, tell the church. If he refuses to listen even to the church, then treat him as you would a Gentile or a tax collector. Amen, I say to you, whatever you bind on earth shall be bound in heaven, and whatever you loose on earth shall be loosed in heaven. Again, amen, I say to you, if two of you agree on earth about anything for which they are to pray, it shall be granted to them by my heavenly Father. For where two or three are gathered together in my name, there am I in the midst of them."

Brief Silence

For Reflection

The heart of this gospel concerning reconciliation is actually about conversion and the call to build up the church. We are all called to bring ourselves and others to conversion and the ongoing challenge to overcome hurts and sinfulness within the community. To "win over" those who "sin . . . against" another in the church is to bring them to turn their life around and become once again faithful members of the community. The work of effecting reconciliation and conversion, however, is not simply the personal judgment of a single community member who has been wronged. The work is always communal, informed by humble prayer, and guided by Jesus who remains "in the midst" of his Body, the church.

We find our deepest identity not in ourselves but in community with God and others. Because of this communal solidarity in Christ, the sin of one member against another affects the life of the whole community of the church. In the church we are accountable to and for one another because our manner of relating, reconciling, and praying together reveals both our commitment to Jesus and his living Presence among us.

✦ When others sin against me, my instinctive reaction is . . . Jesus calls me to respond by . . .

Brief Silence

Prayer

Help us to admit, O good God, that sinning against you and each other weakens the Body of Christ. Help us to have kind and forgiving hearts, to heal any rifts among us, and to foster peace and unity among all people. We ask this through Christ our Lord. **Amen**.

God's merciful forgiveness is generous and assured. As we begin our prayer and reflection, let us call to mind our need for forgiveness . . .

Prayer

How hard it is to forgive a hurt, O God! Yet you forgive us over and over again. Help us to forgive as you do, with hearts open to the other person's dignity and worth. We ask this through Christ our Lord. **Amen**.

Gospel (Matt 18:21-35)

Peter approached Jesus and asked him, "Lord, if my brother sins against me, how often must I forgive? As many as seven times?" Jesus answered, "I say to you, not seven times but seventy-seven times. That is why the kingdom of heaven may be likened to a king who decided to settle accounts with his servants. When he began the accounting, a debtor was brought before him who owed him a huge amount. Since he had no way of paying it back, his master ordered him to be sold, along with his wife, his children, and all his property, in payment of the debt. At that, the servant fell down, did him homage, and said, 'Be patient with me, and I will pay you back in full.' Moved with compassion the master of that servant let him go and forgave him the loan. When that servant had left, he found one of his fellow servants who owed him a much smaller amount. He seized him and started to choke him, demanding, 'Pay back what you owe.' Falling to his knees, his fellow servant begged him, 'Be patient with me, and I will pay you back.' But he refused. Instead, he had the fellow servant put in prison until he paid back the debt. Now when his fellow servants saw what had happened, they were deeply disturbed, and went to their master and reported the whole affair. His master summoned him and said to him, 'You wicked servant! I forgave you your entire debt because you begged me to. Should you not have had pity on your fellow servant, as I had pity on you?' Then in anger his master handed him over to the torturers until he should pay back the whole debt. So will my heavenly Father do to you, unless each of you forgives your brother from your heart."

Brief Silence

For Reflection

Jesus tells a striking parable in this gospel about two instances of forgiveness of debts—one lavishly given, the other miserly withheld. The implication made in the parable is that God acts like the extravagant king. But not so. God's forgiveness of us is always even beyond extravagance, even beyond measure. We measure; God does not. As infinite as God's forgiveness is, to receive it is not without a substantial condition. We are to forgive one another as God forgives—from the heart, "seventy-seven times." Only forgiveness that comes from the heart is immeasurable.

By forgiving we repair the damage to the relationship and restore dignity both to the forgiver and to the forgiven. This is why counting how many times we forgive—even to the seven that Peter suggests at the beginning of the gospel—misses the point. Jesus' response to Peter is a way of reminding us that God forgives us countless times, and this is the motivation for forgiving each other equally countless times. Our "heavenly Father" has shown us the way—forgive one another "from [the] heart."

✦ I offer the bread and cup of compassion and forgiveness in my daily living whenever I . . .

Brief Silence

Prayer

Lord God, we like to count the grievances we have against each other. Not so with you! Grant us the strength to forgive with open hearts, recognizing our own weaknesses and growing in our willingness to beg forgiveness of you and others. We ask this through Christ our Lord. **Amen**.

This gospel tells of a persistent landowner who calls laborers at dawn and throughout the day, and at the end of the day gives all laborers the same wage. Let us ask for God's mercy for the times we have not responded to God's call to labor for the kingdom . . .

Prayer

O God, you persistently hire laborers for the vineyard of salvation. Help us to be persistent in hearing your call, living the Gospel faithfully, and to be grateful for the wages of eternal Life you offer us. We ask this through Christ our Lord. **Amen.**

Gospel (Matt 20:1-16a)

Jesus told his disciples this parable: "The kingdom of heaven is like a landowner who went out at dawn to hire laborers for his vineyard. After agreeing with them for the usual daily wage, he sent them into his vineyard. Going out about nine o'clock, the landowner saw others standing idle in the marketplace, and he said to them, 'You too go into my vineyard, and I will give you what is just.' So they went off. And he went out again around noon, and around three o'clock, and did likewise. Going out about five o'clock, the landowner found others standing around, and said to them, 'Why do you stand here idle all day?' They answered, 'Because no one has hired us.' He said to them, 'You too go into my vineyard.' When it was evening the owner of the vineyard said to his foreman, 'Summon the laborers and give them their pay, beginning with the last and ending with the first.' When those who had started about five o'clock came, each received the usual daily wage. So when the first came, they thought that they would receive more, but each of them also got the usual wage. And on receiving it they grumbled against the landowner, saying, 'These last ones worked only one hour, and you have made them equal to us, who bore the day's burden and the heat.' He said to one of them in reply, 'My friend, I am not cheating you. Did you not agree with me for the usual daily wage? Take what is yours and go. What if I wish to give this last one the same as you? Or am I not free to do as I wish with my own money? Are you envious because I am generous?' Thus, the last will be first, and the first will be last."

Brief Silence

For Reflection

The workers, like the landowner, are persistent. Instead of giving up and going home, they remain in the marketplace seemingly "standing idle." Actually their idleness was not simply doing nothing—theirs was an active waiting; these workers persistently remain ready and willing to work. Of such is the "kingdom of heaven." The "kingdom of heaven" consists of those who persist in awaiting God's recurring call, and who respond willingly no matter what hour the call comes. The last are first not because of the number of hours they work, but because of their openness to God's call no matter when it comes and their faithful response. The "kingdom of heaven" subsists in persistent openness, active waiting, and faithful response. The laborers' wage is beyond monetary expectation—it is salvation.

We might think that the gospel landowner is just to those he called first and generous to those he called last. In fact, our gracious and saving Landowner-God is both just and generous to all the laborers simply because the divine "wages" are always a free gift, undeserved, and more than we can earn or expect. God's "wages" are a share in divine Life.

✦ My manner of distributing Holy Communion witnesses to God's unbounded generosity of "wages" toward all in that . . .

Brief Silence

Prayer

God of the harvest, you offer us salvation when we labor fruitfully to complete the saving work of your Son. Help us to more faithfully make known the message of salvation your Son taught us and one day share fully in the fruit of these labors, the fullness of Life with you. We ask this through Christ our Lord. **Amen**.

Jesus challenges us truly to do the Father's will by living "the way of righteousness." Let us beg God's mercy for the times when we have failed to live according to God's will . . .

Prayer

O God, you ask obedience to your holy will of those who are your beloved people. Help us to discern your will, choose to say yes to whatever you ask of us, and rejoice in our obedience. We ask this through Christ our Lord. **Amen.**

Gospel **(Matt 21:28-32)**

Jesus said to the chief priests and elders of the people: "What is your opinion? A man had two sons. He came to the first and said, 'Son, go out and work in the vineyard today.' He said in reply, 'I will not,' but afterwards changed his mind and went. The man came to the other son and gave the same order. He said in reply, 'Yes, sir,' but did not go. Which of the two did his father's will?" They answered, "The first." Jesus said to them, "Amen, I say to you, tax collectors and prostitutes are entering the kingdom of God before you. When John came to you in the way of righteousness, you did not believe him; but tax collectors and prostitutes did. Yet even when you saw that, you did not later change your minds and believe him."

Brief Silence

For Reflection

Jesus pointedly indicts the "chief priests and elders of the people" by equating them with the second son in this parable who does not do the "father's will." Surprisingly, who does do the "father's will" are "tax collectors and prostitutes." Their sinful lives indicated an initial no to God, but then they came to believe, changed their minds, and repented when they heard a call to "the way of righteousness." Believing is changing our way of living, walking "the way of righteousness," and *doing* the Father's will.

Truth be told, all of us are a little like both sons in the parable. Sometimes we hear and respond faithfully to God's will, but at other times our actions don't carry through what we hear and believe. The good news in this is that God does not change the divine mind about calling us to salvation. Whether we say yes or no to God's call, God does keep calling us. We are the ones who need a change of mind. We are the ones who must believe in God's offer of salvation and faithfully do God's will.

✦ My "Amen" at liturgy becomes a living "yes" to doing God's will when I . . .

Brief Silence

Prayer

God of salvation, doing your will leads us to everlasting happiness with you. When we stray from you, help us to seek the strength and nourishment you offer us to return to fidelity and obedience. We ask this through Christ our Lord. **Amen.**

The tenants of a vineyard kill the landowner's son when he comes to gather the produce. Let us ask for God's mercy for the times we have turned against the divine Son . . .

Prayer

God of judgment and promise, you punish the unfaithful and call the faithful to Life with you. Help us to labor fruitfully in your vineyard by surrendering our self-will to you. We ask this through Christ our Lord. **Amen.**

Gospel (Matt 21:33-43)

Jesus said to the chief priests and the elders of the people: "Hear another parable. There was a landowner who planted a vineyard, put a hedge around it, dug a wine press in it, and built a tower. Then he leased it to tenants and went on a journey. When vintage time drew near, he sent his servants to the tenants to obtain his produce. But the tenants seized the servants and one they beat, another they killed, and a third they stoned. Again he sent other servants, more numerous than the first ones, but they treated them in the same way. Finally, he sent his son to them, thinking, 'They will respect my son.' But when the tenants saw the son, they said to one another, 'This is the heir. Come, let us kill him and acquire his inheritance.' They seized him, threw him out of the vineyard, and killed him. What will the owner of the vineyard do to those tenants when he comes?" They answered him, "He will put those wretched men to a wretched death and lease his vineyard to other tenants who will give him the produce at the proper times." Jesus said to them, "Did you never read in the Scriptures: / *The stone that the builders rejected / has become the cornerstone; / by the Lord has this been done, / and it is wonderful in our eyes?* / Therefore, I say to you, the kingdom of God will be taken away from you and given to a people that will produce its fruit."

Brief Silence

For Reflection

With these words Jesus issues judgment against the chief priests and elders to whom he directs the parable in no uncertain terms: "the kingdom of God will be taken away from you / and given to a people that will produce its fruit." Indeed, the kingdom of God will be taken from anyone who acts egregiously against the norms of righteousness. The chief priests and elders. Even us. It will be given to those who remain faithful to the Son, the Cornerstone. Anyone.

As a metaphor for the kingdom of heaven, it is obvious that the vineyard belongs solely and exclusively to God. Ironically, the vineyard which the wicked tenants attempt to gain by violence is freely given to those of us who will work faithfully to produce its fruit. We are those new tenants who produce fruit because we surrender our self-will to God and accept Jesus as the One who shows the way. By so doing we gain everything. Apart from Jesus we tenants can do nothing on our own, but with Jesus as our Cornerstone we can do anything that is expected of us.

✦ My proclaiming "The Body [Blood] of Christ" calls forth a faithful "Amen" from communicants when I . . .

Brief Silence

Prayer

Gracious God, you invite us to receive the rich vintage of risen Life when we are faithful to you. May we stand up against violence, give others what is rightfully theirs, and never lose sight of the Presence of your risen Son, our cornerstone. We ask this through Christ our Lord. **Amen.**

We are invited to God's banquet to share in the Bread of Life and the wine of salvation. As we begin our time of prayer and reflection, let us come to God with hungry hearts and thirsty souls . . .

Prayer

God of joy and life, you invite us to the rich feast of the eucharistic table. Help us to respond to your invitation with fervor, conscious participation, and readiness to be transformed by you into more perfect members of the Body of Christ. We ask this through Christ our Lord. **Amen.**

Gospel (Matt 22:1-10 [Longer Form: Matt 22:1-14])

Jesus again in reply spoke to the chief priests and elders of the people in parables, saying, "The kingdom of heaven may be likened to a king who gave a wedding feast for his son. He dispatched his servants to summon the invited guests to the feast, but they refused to come. A second time he sent other servants, saying, 'Tell those invited: "Behold, I have prepared my banquet, my calves and fattened cattle are killed, and everything is ready; come to the feast."' Some ignored the invitation and went away, one to his farm, another to his business. The rest laid hold of his servants, mistreated them, and killed them. The king was enraged and sent his troops, destroyed those murderers, and burned their city. Then he said to his servants, 'The feast is ready, but those who were invited were not worthy to come. Go out, therefore, into the main roads and invite to the feast whomever you find.' The servants went out into the streets and gathered all they found, bad and good alike, and the hall was filled with guests."

Brief Silence

For Reflection

Jesus seems to be purposely goading "the chief priests and elders of the people" into angry retaliation for his words of judgment. Jesus is relentless in the message of these parables because of what is at stake: living in the "kingdom of heaven," receiving a judgment for fullness of Life, sharing in the divine wedding feast. Actually, Jesus is purposely goading all of us—not to angry retaliation in response to his judgment, but to change our lives so that we might embrace Life itself. "Many are invited." Only those who respond appropriately "are chosen." Our very Life depends on it.

Even when we refuse to come, our King continually sends out invitations to us. God is relentless in calling us to live in the "kingdom of heaven" and participate in the divine wedding feast. This reminds us of how much God wants to share divine Life and salvation with us. God sent the only Son to live among us and bring us salvation, even at the risk of the Son being killed. God's banquet of Life is worth any cost to God. It ought to be worth any cost to us.

✦ My manner of distributing Holy Communion adds greater joy to the feast when I . . .

Brief Silence

Prayer

Nourishing God, each time we participate in the eucharistic banquet we sit at your wedding feast. Help us to prepare for this grace-filled invitation by living the Gospel ever more faithfully. We ask this through Christ our Lord. **Amen.**

TWENTY-NINTH SUNDAY IN ORDINARY TIME

Jesus is interrogated about what belongs to Caesar and what belongs to God. We seek God's mercy for those times we have not fully given ourselves to God . . .

Prayer

God of unity and love, so often we come to you with divided hearts. Heal us so that we might come to you with transparent hearts living according to the truth of the Gospel. We ask this through Christ our Lord. **Amen**.

Gospel (Matt 22:15-21)

The Pharisees went off and plotted how they might entrap Jesus in speech. They sent their disciples to him, with the Herodians, saying, "Teacher, we know that you are a truthful man and that you teach the way of God in accordance with the truth. And you are not concerned with anyone's opinion, for you do not regard a person's status. Tell us, then, what is your opinion: Is it lawful to pay the census tax to Caesar or not?" Knowing their malice, Jesus said, "Why are you testing me, you hypocrites? Show me the coin that pays the census tax." Then they handed him the Roman coin. He said to them, "Whose image is this and whose inscription?" They replied, "Caesar's." At that he said to them, "Then repay to Caesar what belongs to Caesar and to God what belongs to God."

Brief Silence

For Reflection

There are many deep divisions between "Caesar" and God, between earthly kingdoms and the kingdom of heaven. In this gospel the Pharisees' disciples and the Herodians raise what amounts to a minor division when they raise the question of paying "the census tax to Caesar." Jesus entraps them "with the truth." The "way of God" is not found in opposing civil and religious realms, but in acting as Jesus would in both areas of life, responding appropriately in each "kingdom." Giving ourselves first to God, we will know the "way" and the "truth" of all other loyalties, and our choices and behaviors will further God's plan of salvation.

Jesus quickly dispatches this false divide between realms in which we live, commanding his hearers to give to each realm what properly belongs to it. This is actually the easy part of life. The deepest divide to which we must attend is between disingenuous hearts living a lie and transparent hearts living "in accordance with the truth." This deepest divide is what Jesus came to heal— for those who wish to be healed.

✦ The divisions I experience in daily living are . . . I respond to these divisions by . . .

Brief Silence

Prayer

Heavenly Father, the nourishment we receive at your Son's banquet table strengthens us to know clearly what belongs to you. Help us in our daily living to choose rightly and live according to the Gospel. We ask this through Christ our Lord. **Amen**.

Jesus is quite clear about the greatest commandment of all: love God and neighbor. We are able to love in this way because God has first loved us. We ask God's pardon for the times we have failed in love . . .

Prayer

God of love and life, your commandment to love you with our whole being is expressed through our love for each other. Help us to be open to your grace to live such a worthy commandment. We ask this through Christ our Lord. **Amen.**

Gospel (Matt 22:34-40)

When the Pharisees heard that Jesus had silenced the Sadducees, they gathered together, and one of them, a scholar of the law, tested him by asking, "Teacher, which commandment in the law is the greatest?" He said to him, "You shall love the Lord, your God, with all your heart, with all your soul, and with all your mind. This is the greatest and the first commandment. The second is like it: You shall love your neighbor as yourself. The whole law and the prophets depend on these two commandments."

Brief Silence

For Reflection

To test Jesus the Pharisees questioned him about "which commandment in the law is the greatest." Each Pharisee, no doubt, had some commandment governing religious practice he judged to be the most important. Jesus' answer to the Pharisees takes his hearers beyond any individual commandment or practice to *the* foundation of them all: loving God with one's whole being and loving neighbor as oneself. This is the pervasive, inviolable law. Keeping religious laws—no matter how meticulously—means nothing if the motivation for our actions is not love for God and others. Laws are not entities unto themselves, but always are to lead to the greater good. Keeping laws and precepts—"the whole law and the prophets"—is a way of making visible in our daily living the twofold law of love upon which every commandment is based. Law and love cannot be separated if either is to bring deepened relationships and unity, harmony and justice which are ultimately the goal of both law and love. The law of love is a law of hearts turned toward Other and others.

✦ My love of God becomes "incarnated" as loving service for the Body of Christ whenever I . . .

Brief Silence

Prayer

Lord God, time and again you have shown us the depth of your love for us. May we love others as Jesus showed us how to love, even to giving our all for the good of others. We ask this through Christ our Lord. **Amen.**

As we honor the saints who share
eternal Life with God in heaven,
we rejoice that we share even now
in the divine Life God gives us.
Let us rejoice and be glad in our
blessedness . . .

Prayer

God of salvation, we rejoice in the fidelity of the saints we honor
and join in their everlasting praise of your majesty and glory.
Help us to be faithful to the Gospel, cherish our blessedness, and
one day join all the saints in everlasting Life. We ask this through
Christ our Lord. **Amen**.

Gospel (Matt 5:1-12a)

When Jesus saw the crowds, he went up the mountain, and after
he had sat down, his disciples came to him. He began to teach
them, saying: / "Blessed are the poor in spirit, / for theirs is the Kingdom of heaven. / Blessed are they who mourn, / for they will be
comforted. / Blessed are the meek, / for they will inherit the land. /
Blessed are they who hunger and thirst for righteousness, / for
they will be satisfied. / Blessed are the merciful, / for they will be
shown mercy. / Blessed are the clean of heart, / for they will see
God. / Blessed are the peacemakers, / for they will be called children of God. / Blessed are they who are persecuted for the sake of
righteousness, / for theirs is the Kingdom of heaven. / Blessed are
you when they insult you and persecute you and utter every kind
of evil against you falsely because of me. Rejoice and be glad, for
your reward will be great in heaven."

Brief Silence

For Reflection

The Beatitudes present something of a "which comes first, the chicken or the egg" situation. Are we blessed because we live and act in a certain way, or does God's gift of blessedness bestowed so generously on us enable us to live and act in a Godlike way? At first glance, the Beatitudes seem to say that blessedness is a reward given to those who live and act in ways that transcend the ways of the world. In reality, we are able to live and act in these ways of the Beatitudes because we are *already* blessed. As children of God through our baptism, blessedness is who we are (unless we consciously deny it through sin). Because we are already blessed, we live and act as God does. Because we are already blessed, we live even now in "the kingdom of heaven." Blessedness is a way of being that stretches us toward what we become in the fullness of Life. Being blessed is God's gift to us; choosing to live our blessedness is our gift to God and each other.

✦ The saint who best models the Beatitudes for me is . . . This saint challenges me to . . . This saint helps me by . . .

Brief Silence

Prayer

God of blessings, you shower us with every good gift. Strengthen us to be worthy of the holiness to which you call us and one day to share the everlasting happiness of the fullness of Life. We ask this through Christ our Lord. **Amen**.

We remember during November in a special way our loved ones who have died. Let us open ourselves to God's promise of eternal Life for those who are faithful . . .

Prayer

God of salvation and peace, we come to you with hearts filled with hope, knowing that your divine Son does not reject anyone who comes to him. Keep us close to you, faithful to doing your will, and grant us the grace to be faithful as those we remember this month. We ask this through Christ our Lord. **Amen**.

Gospel (John 6:37-40 [see p. 125 for other gospel options])

Jesus said to the crowds: "Everything that the Father gives me will come to me, and I will not reject anyone who comes to me, because I came down from heaven not to do my own will but the will of the one who sent me. And this is the will of the one who sent me, that I should not lose anything of what he gave me, but that I should raise it on the last day. For this is the will of my Father, that everyone who sees the Son and believes in him may have eternal life, and I shall raise him up on the last day."

Brief Silence

For Reflection

We have good reason to call this day a festival of the "faithful" departed. While our deceased loved ones were not perfect in their

lives here on earth—none of us is—we also know them to have
been good people who tried to live good lives. Failures do not keep
us from eternal Life; refusal to seek forgiveness and mercy will.
We have hope that Jesus will not lose any one of the faithful but
they will join in the glory of eternal Life.

Yes, this is a festival of hope! Hope is not empty; it is based on
God's fidelity, mercy, forgiveness, compassion, and love that have
been consistently and freely given us since the very beginning of
creation. Jesus chooses to own us, to possess us, to attach us to his
Sacred Heart. We belong to One who will never let go of us. The
one stipulation is that, like Jesus, his followers do the will of the
Father. Those faithful departed whom we remember this day are
not lost—they have believed in Jesus, they have done the will of
God, they have gained eternal Life.

✦ Some ways I remember and reverence my deceased loved
ones are . . .

Brief Silence

Prayer

God of comfort, your Son Jesus spoke words of hope and life,
promising that he will not reject anyone who comes to him.
Through the nourishment we seek by participating in the eucharistic banquet, strengthen us to remain faithful and one day join
our loved ones in everlasting praise of you. We ask this through
Christ our Lord. **Amen**.

Other gospel options for November 2:
Matthew 5:1-12a / Matthew 11:25-30 / Matthew 25:31-46 /
Luke 7:11-17 / Luke 23:44-46, 50, 52-53; 24:1-6a / Luke 24:13-16,
28-35 / John 5:24-29 / John 6:51-58 / John 11:17-27 / John 11:32-45 /
John 14:1-6

Jesus challenges his disciples to put into practice what they preach. As we begin our prayer and reflection, let us recall those times when our actions have not matched our words . . .

Prayer

O God, your word is sure and always accomplishes what you say. Help us not simply to speak words of salvation to others, but to live Gospel values in all we do, thus preaching by our doing. We ask this through Christ our Lord. **Amen**.

Gospel (Matt 23:1-12)

Jesus spoke to the crowds and to his disciples, saying, "The scribes and the Pharisees have taken their seat on the chair of Moses. Therefore, do and observe all things whatsoever they tell you, but do not follow their example. For they preach but they do not practice. They tie up heavy burdens hard to carry and lay them on people's shoulders, but they will not lift a finger to move them. All their works are performed to be seen. They widen their phylacteries and lengthen their tassels. They love places of honor at banquets, seats of honor in synagogues, greetings in market-places, and the salutation 'Rabbi.' As for you, do not be called 'Rabbi.' You have but one teacher, and you are all brothers. Call no one on earth your father; you have but one Father in heaven. Do not be called 'Master'; you have but one master, the Christ. The greatest among you must be your servant. Whoever exalts himself will be humbled; but whoever humbles himself will be exalted."

Brief Silence

For Reflection

Our words and deeds—our word-behaviors—must reveal our ultimate word-behavior: that we are disciples of Jesus, the servant of others. To be a humble servant is simply living in right relationship with God and others. This means that we never forget our first and most important title, which is not to be teacher or master, but to be humble servant. This means that we practice what we preach. And what we preach is Jesus, who is humble servant now exalted.

In very clear terms Jesus condemns the "scribes and Pharisees" for the way they act. They don't practice what they preach and they relish titles but do not live up to the demands these titles place upon them. Both these ways of acting reveal a corrupted disposition toward God and God's people. Then Jesus admonishes "the crowd" and "the disciples" to focus on him and him alone as the true teacher and master. He is true Teacher and Master in showing us how to be servant of all: he humbled himself. For this, he is exalted by his Father. *How* he is truly reveals *who* he is. *How* we are reveals us to be . . .

✦ I know I have failed to practice what I preach when . . . The strongest preaching I do by the way I live is . . .

Brief Silence

Prayer

God of wisdom and truth, you sent your Son to live among us and be our Teacher and Master. Help us to follow faithfully in his footsteps, that our actions might proclaim the humble servant-love in our hearts. We ask this through Christ our Lord. **Amen.**

This gospel tells the parable of the five wise virgins who have enough oil for their lamps and five foolish virgins who do not. Let us pray and ponder how well we are prepared to meet Christ our Bridegroom . . .

Prayer

God of salvation, we do not know the day or hour when your divine Son will return to gather all things back to you. Help us to prepare by the way we live the Gospel and instill in our hearts the confidence that we need not fear his coming. We ask this through Christ our Lord. **Amen**.

Gospel (Matt 25:1-13)

Jesus told his disciples this parable: "The kingdom of heaven will be like ten virgins who took their lamps and went out to meet the bridegroom. Five of them were foolish and five were wise. The foolish ones, when taking their lamps, brought no oil with them, but the wise brought flasks of oil with their lamps. Since the bridegroom was long delayed, they all became drowsy and fell asleep. At midnight, there was a cry, 'Behold, the bridegroom! Come out to meet him!' Then all those virgins got up and trimmed their lamps. The foolish ones said to the wise, 'Give us some of your oil, for our lamps are going out.' But the wise ones replied, 'No, for there may not be enough for us and you. Go instead to the merchants and buy some for yourselves.' While they went off to buy it, the bridegroom came and those who were ready went into the wedding feast with him. Then the door was locked. Afterwards the other virgins came and said, 'Lord, Lord, open the door for us!' But he said in reply, 'Amen, I say to you, I do not know you.' Therefore, stay awake, for you know neither the day nor the hour."

Brief Silence

For Reflection

This parable is fraught with symbolic images of light, delay, waiting, drowsiness and sleep, a cry, midnight darkness, arrival, wedding feast, some admitted some are not. All these images turn our attention to the Second Coming of Christ, our own waiting in this in-between time of living in both light and darkness, the reality that some will be admitted to the heavenly banquet and some will not, the necessity of being known by Christ and being prepared for his coming. Wait we must, but this waiting is not inactive or empty. How we spend this waiting time determines how we will spend the rest of time.

There is no doubt that the Bridegroom will come. What is unexpected is his *long delay* which Matthew is specifically addressing. The question for us, then, is how do we deal with the delay? How do we live in the in-between time of now and what is to come? Matthew is suggesting an issue beyond vigilance—that we must also *be prepared*. We are living in a crucial time of spending our lives being open to Christ's comings in the here and now.

✦ Holy Communion is already a participation in the Bridegroom's wedding feast because . . .

Brief Silence

Prayer

O God, we seek you, we long for you, we hope for your Presence and love. During this time of waiting for Christ's Second Coming, help us to prepare well for the everlasting feast to which you call us and awaits those who are faithful. We ask this through Christ our Lord. **Amen**.

Jesus speaks of a master who entrusts his possessions to his servants and demands an accounting from them when he returns from a journey. Let us ask ourselves how well we have used the possessions God has given us . . .

Prayer

Gracious God, you have given us all we need to be good and faithful servants of your divine Son. Strengthen us as we strive to use the gifts we have been given for the good of others. We ask this through Christ our Lord. **Amen.**

Gospel **(Matt 25:14-30 [Shorter Form: Matt 25:14-15, 19-21])**

Jesus told his disciples this parable: "A man going on a journey called in his servants and entrusted his possessions to them. To one he gave five talents; to another, two; to a third, one—to each according to his ability. Then he went away. Immediately the one who received five talents went and traded with them, and made another five. Likewise, the one who received two made another two. But the man who received one went off and dug a hole in the ground and buried his master's money.

"After a long time the master of those servants came back and settled accounts with them. The one who had received five talents came forward bringing the additional five. He said, 'Master, you gave me five talents. See, I have made five more.' His master said to him, 'Well done, my good and faithful servant. Since you were faithful in small matters, I will give you great responsibilities. Come, share your master's joy.' Then the one who had received two talents also came forward and said, 'Master, you gave me two

talents. See, I have made two more.' His master said to him, 'Well
done, my good and faithful servant. Since you were faithful in
small matters, I will give you great responsibilities. Come, share
your master's joy.' Then the one who had received the one talent
came forward and said, 'Master, I knew you were a demanding
person, harvesting where you did not plant and gathering where
you did not scatter; so out of fear I went off and buried your talent in the ground. Here it is back.' His master said to him in reply,
'You wicked, lazy servant! So you knew that I harvest where I did
not plant and gather where I did not scatter? Should you not then
have put my money in the bank so that I could have got it back
with interest on my return? Now then! Take the talent from him
and give it to the one with ten. For to everyone who has, more will
be given and he will grow rich; but from the one who has not, even
what he has will be taken away. And throw this useless servant
into the darkness outside, where there will be wailing and grinding of teeth.'"

Brief Silence

For Reflection

The most important choice we make in life is fidelity to whatever we are called to do. The continuation of Jesus' saving work
depends upon this fidelity. We are now living in the delay before
our Master's return. This parable teaches what to do during this
time of waiting—it is not empty time, for sure. We are to live in
such a way that we grow in our greatest "possession"—the divine
Life that has been given us. If, like the lazy servant in the parable,
we focus on our fear and Christ's judgment, we will be paralyzed
in our ability to continue using the "investments" we have been
given to continue Christ's work of salvation. However, if we focus
on the promised share in the "master's joy," then we will be willing
to risk what we have in order to grow in our most prized possession—our share in divine Life and the relationship with Christ
that entails. The Christian life and journey of discipleship begins
with our being given an unmerited share in God's Life. When we

are faithful it will end wondrously—we will enter fully into the "master's joy."

✦ Jesus, the Master, has entrusted to me these "possessions" . . . I use them to . . .

Brief Silence

Prayer

Loving God, you fill us with the joy of your Life and goodness. Help us to be faithful servants who one day will share in everlasting joy and Life with you. We ask this through Christ our Lord. **Amen**.

We honor Christ the King who is enthroned in eternal glory. Let us open our hearts to being counted among his blessed ones . . .

Prayer

God our benevolent King, you rule justly and offer peace to those who follow your commands. Help us to reach out to others with the generosity, kindness, and blessings you have so lavishly bestowed on us. We ask this through Christ our Lord. **Amen**.

Gospel (Matt 25:31-46)

Jesus said to his disciples: "When the Son of Man comes in his glory, and all the angels with him, he will sit upon his glorious throne, and all the nations will be assembled before him. And he will separate them one from another, as a shepherd separates the sheep from the goats. He will place the sheep on his right and the goats on his left. Then the king will say to those on his right, 'Come, you who are blessed by my Father. Inherit the kingdom prepared for you from the foundation of the world. For I was hungry and you gave me food, I was thirsty and you gave me drink, a stranger and you welcomed me, naked and you clothed me, ill and you cared for me, in prison and you visited me.' Then the righteous will answer him and say, 'Lord, when did we see you hungry and feed you, or thirsty and give you drink? When did we see you a stranger and welcome you, or naked and clothe you? When did we see you ill or in prison, and visit you?' And the king will say to them in reply, 'Amen, I say to you, whatever you

did for one of the least brothers of mine, you did for me.' Then he
will say to those on his left, 'Depart from me, you accursed, into
the eternal fire prepared for the devil and his angels. For I was
hungry and you gave me no food, I was thirsty and you gave me
no drink, a stranger and you gave me no welcome, naked and you
gave me no clothing, ill and in prison, and you did not care for
me.' Then they will answer and say, 'Lord, when did we see you
hungry or thirsty or a stranger or naked or ill or in prison, and
not minister to your needs?' He will answer them, 'Amen, I say to
you, what you did not do for one of these least ones, you did not
do for me.' And these will go off to eternal punishment, but the
righteous to eternal life."

Brief Silence

For Reflection

No greater honor can we give our Savior-King than to serve him
in one another. In a sense, then, our focus on each other is really a
focus on Christ—for it is a measure of how much we imitate his
care for others. It is a measure of how much we are his faithful
disciples. He showed us by his very life how to care for others. So
must we spend our lives in this way.

Christ the King *will* come "in his glory." It is not "if" he will
come, but "when." There is an imperative in the immediacy of this
"when." The gospel claim is clear: Christ the King, arrayed in all
his glory, is present *now* in the other. We must look beyond what
we see with our eyes and see with the heart of Christ; we must see
others as he sees them. His throne is the person of the other; he
dwells within them. The "when" of his coming is now. The kingdom of God is now. The judgment is now. In our care for others
here and now, Christ the King reigns.

✦ When I take time to reflect on Christ coming in all his glory,
I am moved to . . .

Brief Silence

OUR LORD JESUS CHRIST, KING OF THE UNIVERSE

Prayer

Heavenly Father, at the end of time your Son will come arrayed in all his glory. May we live the Gospel in such a faithful way that we eagerly look for his coming, have no fear of final judgment, and one day come to share the fullness of Life with Christ our King. We ask this through Christ our Lord. **Amen**.

My Body Tells
Its Own Story

My Body Tells
Its Own Story

Poems by Mary Zeppa

Cherry Grove Collections

Published by Cherry Grove Collections
P.O. Box 541106
Cincinnati, OH 45254-1106

ISBN: 9781625491268
LCCN: 2015933210

Poetry Editor: Kevin Walzer
Business Editor: Lori Jareo

Visit us on the web at www.cherry-grove.com

Cover design by Laura Martin
Cover photograph by Anita Frimkess Fein
Cover art, *Solitude,* by Laura Hohlwein

for Norm and Mary, whose love I embody,
and for Manny

Acknowledgments

These poems, sometimes in earlier versions, first appeared in the following journals and anthologies:

I Am Becoming the Woman I Wanted (Papier-Mache Press, 1994): "Osteoporosis"

Landing Signals: An Anthology of Sacramento Poets (Sacramento Poetry Center, 1985): "Explaining to a Man," "Henry and Anna and Love"

Medusa's Kitchen: "For heavy lifting"

One (Dog) Press: "Navigable Sorrow," "Writing to Gertrude Stein While Wearing My T-Shirt From the New York City Ballet"

one/dog/press: "Lovemaking, #1"

Perihelion: "The Begotten," "Bilateral Equation," "God's Messengers," "Swimming Up, Out of Such Dreams"

Poetry Now: "The High Lonesome," "Let beauty change us," "The Lit Globe of Her Inner Life"

Putah Creek: "The Blood-Is-Thicker-Than-Vodka Brother"

Quercus: "The body makes love possible," "Explaining to a Man," "Loss," "Tide Pool"

Suisun Valley Review: "Abstraction"

Telescope: "October Light"

Tule Review: "Apparently, I am afraid of dying," "The Little Notebooks of Anna Magdalena Bach: A Coda," "A Living Will"

The following poems, some in earlier versions, appeared in the 2005 Rattlesnake Press limited edition chapbook *The Battered Bride Overture:* "The Battered Bride Overture," "Clara Schumann's last winter as Wife," "How They Hear Us All Coming," "Just an old broken nightmare, " "A Living Will," "October Light," "Osteoporosis," "Say, *I don't remember,*" "To be a woman:," "Where the Apple Falls."

The following poems appeared in the 2002 Poets Corner Press limited edition chapbook *Little Ship of Blessing:* "The Lit Globe of Her Inner Life," "The Little Notebooks of Anna Magdalena Bach: A Coda," "Loss."

Contents

I

Abstraction

for Georgia O'Keeffe, who wanted a child

1

She managed the sky:

hip sockets framing
surrounding
the blue

stopped only by
the canvas, the frame.

2

But the skull that is barrenness
floats on white canvas.
Eye sockets taking
in all that they can

cheekbone and jawbone
and thin
yellow petal

thickness
of cloud, floating island

of blue

and red hills and red hills
the curves of
the red hills

that reach out
to cradle the sky.

The body makes love possible

Galway Kinnell

Without flesh, the spirit
is desperate, circles and tries
to be weightless, be air,
be wind that can only
caress what is shapely
and hold nothing, take
nothing back.

The Little Notebooks of
Anna Magdalena Bach: A Coda

The body an alien we rent a room in. "I don't get
this mind-body thing," said the funny man. "The brain's
in the body, last time I looked." Ah, but the brain

is merely the furniture to house the abstraction
that hungers for saffron, that longs to be
Van Gogh's good ear. That cocks that ear,

bends it toward her soprano: Anna Magdalena
stirs Widower Bach, raises the hairs on the back
of his neck. I'd be their first baby: warm, wet

and living, who dropped into Bach's waiting
hands. Yes, life will come back for us, turning
the carriage round, stopping the jet on a dime.

The Lit Globe of Her Inner Life

Her hands in her cat's fur, rose petals,
son's hair. In the bread dough, the 6-a.m.-
windowpane-sunshine. Gives her finger

print, lip print, sweet scent, deep breath.
Hums the melody nobody knows. Made
of lump in throat, goose bumps, hot surge

of blue. Made of mezzo-soprano and
meadowlark and the tick of a lazy-day clock.
Made of blood and bone: dance of the Magi.

Made of maiden alone by the brook, made
of leaping fish meeting the pelican's bill,
made of scorn on the face of the gull.

Made of scarecrow, and scared boy,
and wings of the bat as it startles
its way through the night.

Made of every egg empty and broken,
made of story of nobody's life. Made
of chicken who rhumbaed across

the road. Made of savior on
waterwings, ghost of a chance,
made of son of the Sunday noon nap.

Lovemaking #1

Always two bodies
asking the questions:

the hands, the hips,
the fur along the thighs.

Two bodies inventing
a story beginning:

and the stone rolled away from the cave.

Loss

Loss, loss, loss, there is no other story.
—Robert Hass

There's no great loss without some little gain.
—Caroline Ingalls

for Stephen Hawking, Michel Petruccianni
and the girl with the bright silver eyes

1

So the world slips away from us, freeing
our hands. The child who will never
be born
       is dancing before me, her silver eyes shining,
an actual, flesh-and-blood child
                  is spinning, is whirling. This
daughter
of strangers, her flesh bright
with my secret song.

2

The orbits of planets and wheelchairs.
The lights of the stars and the mind.
A man in a thin, collapsed body

the silence will never contain. The weight
of the heart and the brain cells. The balance
of living and time. Of grey matter:

porous, absorbing
the theory, translating
the pores of the skin

into meteor, memory, tentative
star. The eyes
catch the fire and shine.

3

And the music the spheres still remember,
that balance the silence
implies,
      that music
spins out of a body
the size of a 6-year-old child.

Though his stunted legs dangle,
his strong arms hold on
to the young wife who carries him,

bed to piano, who leans in to taste
one last kiss, who moves through
the spheres
         he spins out of the sounds
that flood through
his marrow, his hands.

4

When the body I love is a memory,
a slow ache in fingertips, thighs,

when absence gives up its definite
shape, when it pushes my clinging arms wide,

when you are a ghost in the bloodstream,
constriction beneath the last rib,

I shall reach for a shadow,
blow dust from its mouth,

begin again, start
with life's kiss.

Lovemaking #2

The brain leaves its Gordian
knot on the pillow. The body
laughs all the way home.

The Meaning of *Broucha*

In Hebrew, they call your name blessing.
This is a given, of course. But, in Spanish,
Bruja becomes witch. How could it be

otherwise? So, *Broucha-Bruja,* snap
your gnarled fingers: a gossamer
canopy blooms and makes us all

witnesses *(Cry, little bride!)*
at the wedding of Broucha
and Abraham Isaac,

18 years before I was born.
Oh, beauty, such cheekbones.
We watch your spine straighten,

we watch your hands open and arc.
Watch your slender fingers reach out
for him, gather him up with your doubts.

The Momentary Immortal

Beauty is momentary in the mind—
The fitful tracing of a portal;
But in the flesh it is immortal.
—Wallace Stevens

That visceral wonder. That intake of breath.
Is beauty her cheekbones? Is beauty his mouth?

The curve of an ankle Great-Grandfather
glimpsed 'neath the flare of a crinolined skirt?

From that scant inch of flesh, he imagined
a woman so rosy and firm, she warmed

61 years of long nights with a timorous,
sad, sloe-eyed wife who sighed for

the postman, a man with the face
of a Greek and beneficent god.

Stela: 32nd Anniversary

for Bob Zeppa

You still float up out of my night-skull.
Beg me, today of all days, to keep watch
out our forgotten window for the tilt
of your orange beret. Heart attack.
Cremated, scattered. History,
those brown, sculpted thighs. Still,
last night, they carried you out our
front door, off our porch, down

our crumbling stairs, and into our yard
where star jasmine trapped crabgrass
and red maple leaves. You still housekept,
read Gibbon at breakfast, still couldn't cook
pretty food. Remember that gunmetal gray
bouillabaisse? Delicious, once we closed our eyes.

Writing to Gertrude Stein While Wearing My T-Shirt from the New York City Ballet

for Claire

Dear Gertrude Stein,
The sun is the sun and the twain
always meet. The dancers who vault
my chest leap into darkness. Still, their dresses
are blue and are long. Thus, their heels are invisible,
toes merely someplace to rise from. You, only you,

understand. Like Paris, like Alice's kitchen,
the place where the brownies were baked.
In her sugar-sweet arms, you began
your beguine while she licked
your chocolate mustache.
Then her tongue,

that hot firefly, darted
for your center, your red, open
mouth. So, pity Picasso who leapt to
their rescue: his clowns gazing down on
your bath. For you hung them, they say, on
those damp walls, to gaze on as you and she rode

through the bath, through the bubble bath Hermes sent up
each Friday night of your life. Cerulean bubbles for Alice
(a river otter, a seal) to glide through to you, my
stout General, just off the boat from Minsk,
Vladivostok, from Oakland, anywhere
empty and cold.

Explaining to a Man

Imagine cramps in your penis.
Imagine tight
squeezing pain.
Imagine watching
the raw swollen head
for the first sign of real blood.

A drop first.
A trickle.
A clot.
And then
the thick
oozing flood.

This is the no life
they say isn't death.
The no life, the red
emptiness.

How easily
it slips away.
So quick
you can't hold it back.

Apparently, I am afraid of dying

Broucha Abrams, 95

She beat us to this place,
tongue barbed as wire, mean
as a grandmother snake. Now,

she's hollow-cheeked, dentures
in hiding. I'm her mirror, her
have-pity face. Flesh has us both

cornered. She's stuck in that chair
and I am her daughter-in-law.
"I am panicky, loose from my body."

Breast milk and blood and his duty:
my husband, her only child, slumped
beside me and sinking fast into his spine,

into his crumpled-paper-bag skin.
"Apparently, I am afraid of dying."
Is that her own shadow rustling?

Or a dead husband slithering close?
His cold breath in her ear, on the back
of her neck, in the hiding place under

her breasts, where they nestle,
her aborted daughters, in their
pink-and-white swaddling clothes.

In the Baths, I Remember

What I never understood, losing you, old friend,
was how those orgies began. You, who loved
only men, craving Carol's lush skin,
touching, stroking her, trembling and
rosy while her husband cheered:
"There! Yes! Yes! More!"

Or how you locked into your triad,
how you made the Beast with Three Backs,
made the six-legged Beast thunder over
the finish line where Carol
would whinny, toss her red mane
while you and Doug licked her wet flanks.

In the Baths, I remember
those silk waves, your black hair
and your lean build: all shoulders, no waist.
How those crooked teeth flashed in your lush mouth,
as your baritone aria shook the city:
"Hunger! Joy! Nothing to lose!"

The Letter That Won't Leave Her Pen

Dorogaya, the life I earned wrestles this body.
This skull cheats. These fingers don't grasp.

Hands, faces, rivers: these eyes blur.
96 years shudder past. *Dorogaya,*
in dreams, I live

young and in houses
built of washed, indigo stones,

walk the hills of Jerusalem,
my father's hand in mine,
my son a blush under my skin.

Dorogaya, he leaps in me,
unborn and tender, tapping

this belly's taut drum.
And my hands fill
with gentians. And silence

stays prayerful
and under my tongue.

Let beauty change us

forever. Let our spines straighten, our eyes
fasten upon God's big, beautiful face,
on the pearl it is in His broad hands.

God leans lightly on both sturdy elbows,
letting our day's light drift in
through the open top half

of His favorite Dutch door.
Van Gogh painted it
Japanese red. Van Gogh

leaned on it
100 mornings: *Would
this light give him*

its grace? God's untroubled
this morning and smiling: His
countenance radiates.

My Body Tells Its Own Story

At 112 pounds, taut and contained, I
was a Minimalist. And that standard,

each rib its own masterpiece,
mocks me from albums, from dreams.

It's history now, the sensation
of just-enough over the bones.

Like the cave art the ovaries painted
on the walls of what's left of the womb.

My Day of Atonement

for Broucha at *Yortzeit*

You are memory now, disembodied
under grass under an olive tree
on a slope overlooking Los Angeles,
in the plot-that-had-not-changed-a-bit.

Pity the shiksa who laid you there.
Who was led *(Vey iz mir!)* into sin, into
breaking the laws of your fathers by
the man from the funeral home.

The red-headed man in the yarmulke,
taking charge, stepping out of the hearse.
"Would you like to see her?" he offered.
No, I said first and then, *Yes*. And he

unlatched your casket and unwrapped
your veil. For comfort. Forgive me,
I saw you: rouged, rosy,
ready for G-d.

Say, *I don't remember*

and it all comes back to you:
the red concertina, his hands:
their thick stubby fingers,
the hairs on his knuckles
alight in the glow of the lamp.

Say, *I don't remember* and it all floods back:
his hands at your shoulders, your waist
as you stood at the sink, with your
hands deep in suds, with his
whispering tongue on your throat.

Say, *I've forgotten* and it's your new movie:
his long index finger dipped into you,
the hot, scarlet cross that he made,
up your ribcage, across

the white slopes of your breasts.
Your blood drying, sticky and tender
and the trace of it 20 years after
in the air, in the sign of the cross.

II

What Else We Know

Down the aisle at Long's, I spot
the composer's wife clutching
her brown, battered purse.

Through the drugstore, I follow
her mind as it wanders: to him
at home with his nurse *where he*

sleeps a lot, isn't in any pain, laughs
in C major, as always, reaches
for me with his voice.

A matter of weeks: a brain
tumor. Which the doc drilled,
snipped, sliced, lifted clean

but for one small knot caught
in the music that's left: a deep song
that swells from the spine.

Letter to Dad, Posthumous

Dear Dad,

Are your molecules spinning? Been a year full
of tumbles and spins since you gave up
the ghost, found an orbit
out of body and free of your sins.

Still, when, O! holy Lutheran morning,
Mom falls on her gardener's knees
on the new-mown grass of your
prickly grave, she thinks it's you

tickling her right through
the pantyhose she quite forgot
when, with trowel and pink bucket
of lilies, she knelt to spruce up your plot.

So she seizes it, your playful moment,
to let fall some family news: *our new
café-au-lait great-granddaughter,
our handsome, black grandson-out-law.*

And, she whispers it quickly, *our fine son
is teetering over the brink, run amok
with a bottle of vodka, tearing out
a deep root in my heart.* Then, she's up,

pushing off with the flat of her hand.
But she leans down to stroke it,
that prickly grass, as if
it were your crew-cut head.

Osteoporosis

Morbid absorption of bony substance
to which small-boned women
are particularly prone.

For a woman's small bones
may turn brittle
and a woman's thin spine

may turn mean, may say *No*
to the burden her flesh makes
once the long downslide

begins. For once the skeleton
starts its good-byes, and once
the slow creaking starts,

once the hot roses flash
—belly, breasts, face—
it's the slick-with-sweat shine

of hot flesh melting down
while the battered, defiant, old heart
pumps the pound-foolish blood

toward the catch in the throat
for the quick and the dead
and the lost.

To be a woman:

hollow at center,
honeycomb, vessel,
the mouth of the cave

or

to be empty: an echo,
a chasm, a skull broken
open, spilled honey for flies.

36th Birthday

for Norman, my father
and for my mother, Mary Rose

Still proof of the gleam in my father's blue eyes:
your daughter,
the cells of your cells

conceived in your boardinghouse
on fresh percale
under your plaid counterpane.

Rising and falling,
your bodies all grace
again and again and again

the sweat and the semen
a cool, mingled stain
the sweet taste of salt on her face.

Her head finds its place
on your shoulder: your wife
settling down in your arms,

my mother who sleeps
on those blue, tumbled sheets
a white rose, an opening bloom.

Where the Apple Falls

My sister's voice is calm traveling 3,000 miles.
It's history: her husband slamming her
into walls, hurling her out of doors,
locking their only phone in his van.

Our family beauty: those huge blue eyes,
those 95 curvy pounds. And that wry,
that whiskey-cigarette voice

they all recognize at the hotline,
well trained to triage, to spot:
those voices whose timbre

says *martyr*. Her
husband of 22 years
told her how sick *she* is,

threatened *To ream you out
a new asshole. Sack
of shit! Loser!*

he screamed at
their four kids. Sharp,
interchangeable names.

What an arm! How he
lofted her: personal
best. Record time

from the launch to
the landing, to those
practiced, rapid-fire jabs.

**

Once there were bruises
the shapes of fingers
braceleting my upper arms.

Our mother's body still
says *Endure.* She is
a midnight-kitchen-

floor-scrubber,
a whistler of
angry tunes.

***

"When you were a twinkle
in your father's eye."
Consequence

wearing a skin. And my
sister's sons took it all in,
while their sister dialed 911.

A Living Will

Here, take what's left of sunlight: these shadows
on my walls, these yesterdays in corners,
these dust-mote reveries. To you,

I leave the echoes that crowd around
my bones: sonatas, waltzes, lowdown
blues and small tunes with no names.

I open out a diorama, fold it from the spine.
First memory: red metal swing suffused
by golden sun. A child swings out

to meet the light. Their shadows
draw her close. The dead are here
beside us: in our voices, in our touch.

The music plays us all it knows: the slow
laments, the hymns, the intermittent joy,
the steady hunger trapped in bones.

Kaleidoscope Magic

It's all done with mirrors.
My body in your arms

a breast or a hip or a thigh
at the edge of a circle

your fingers keep turning
away and away and away.

Death Tolls, October '96

14-year-old at the end of a noose, growing cold
in her mother's garage. Down the aisle, her white

coffin: pink garlands of roses. Sweets to
the desperate sweet. For the 19-year-old in

the head-on (sirens and daring and speed), we
meditate, read the Book of the Dead, study photos:

his grin and his grace. 36 and the coroner
"can't say for sure." "An accidental

overdose," says his mother's choked
telephone voice. And Grandma

turns 93 (once Queen of the Kibbutz,
third smile from the right, a beauty

with bobbed raven hair). Her face
is a monument: pogroms, Ellis Island,

manic depression, divorce. Death
is a window and we're on

the scenic route. Whistling
Blackbird, bye-bye in the dark.

The Begotten

In the dream, the fat baby, soft as our last wish,
powdery, warm in my arms. And solid, as real
as tomorrow, cradled and passed hand to hand.

It's the top of her head we keep kissing: fresh, sweet
and rich in the nose. We are millionaire misers,
a phalanx and tender. Our voices, at last,

reach to God. Yet, in the next scene, we are prisoners:
concentration camp: shuddering, naked. Terror
leaks out of our eyes. We all know

where we're going. Even the baby for whom
we would all leap through fire as we must for we see
the smoke (silver-white, plumy) rising up to the edge
   of our cliff.

The Lords at the edge of tomorrow still number

all that you borrowed, you stole. Only you
know what still remains hidden. Where
the bodies lie, under what soil.

How A Memory Makes Itself Known

It floats up from the cache in my bloodstream.
It draws breath to remind flesh and bone
we began as this red-headed lassie
playing *Skip to my Lou* with her mom.

Skip, skip, skip to my Lou! is my
reedy 4-year-old song till my
out-of-breath skipping mother
scoops me up, skips me on

home. Of all the fingers
that touched me: my mother's
unblemished, soft, young,
in their own revery

of my father's smooth face
as it was that last night
before he shipped out when I
already jumped in her womb.

Swimming Up, Out of Such Dreams

In the morning, I loft myself over my body

wishing for 20 more years
in the other direction: 45, 35, letting

the ovaries choose. In the belly
of any beast heavy with longing,

leaps the ghost of a ghost of a chance.

Tide Pool

Flat fish the color
of crumbling sand, green crabs the size
of my thumb. How desperate
they are under our cool eyes. We peer
from a great height, from some
starving planet where hunger
has come to mean love.

Martha, at Ease by the Lap Pool

She pretends to read,
scanning her silk, scarlet lap
as her daughter slides into
cool, blue waves,
adjusting

her pink, flowered cap.
The girl's clumsy on land like a dolphin
with its flippers disabled by sand.
Eliza, the girl who is 40,
who is striking

that come-hither pose, looking
over her round, luscious
shoulder, rosy mouth
in a sexpot's
soft pout.

In this pool, up this lap,
her brown arms flash. Eliza
swims, grinning for joy
while her mother
pretends she

is reading
that flat box
of pages, her book.
In this radiant,
shimmering

hot light,
the mother in her
slips away. For this
hour, in this sunlight,
she's Martha:

the tomboy
who flew
through the trees.
In her own arms,
the strength to swing

surges. She propels herself
back: she is 10,
swinging elm to elm
down that lane: that rented
farm where Dorcas,

her mother,
climbs down
battered steps into
white, blistering noon.
Dorcas lifts up her eyes, scans

the long sway, the ripple
of those rustling trees
for a flash of her daughter,
her Martha. Dear God,
how their laughter would rise.

The Suicide's Life Lets Him Down

Ann clambers the tree's trunk to cut her son down,
tug his blond body out of those branches.

Her Absalom's long, wavy hair wraps her round,
entangles with her hair, flows over

their shoulders. His white, narrow feet will swing
over the roses

till her shuddering
hands cut him loose.

For heavy lifting:

a lever. For nights that won't end:
a scream. For deep-in-the-heartbreak where-

no-one-can-follow: a miner's torch,
steady beam. For old wounds:

an implacable needle. Tie that binds
with its raggedy thread. And

your old eagle eye for as long
as it takes. You're

the rescue squad:
bend your sweet head.

III

Gravity

What gravity steals
is the space in our bones.
And we who miss it most sing.
—Theory

That handsome lad, Sophocles, too young
to fight, sang in the victory choir. Stood
sentinel tall in the back row, his shoulders

agreeably wide. At his clarion tenor flew open
the eyes of old women in black, left behind
on their perch on the catacomb walls

to watch the dust gather them in. But gravity
squats on the hump of her back. She's 95, goin'
down slow with her *pekl* of *tsuris* evolving:

a no-relief map of her world. Tears swallow up
newsprint and all of her books. Her telephone
hisses and spits. Her diaper leaks onto

her wheelchair. Her intercom sends its regrets.
"Assisted living," they call it. Where
the "smart-mouth aides" must cut her meat.

Where she's showered on Tuesdays and Fridays.
Where she's "panicky" at 5 a.m. Where she's
The Old Woman Who Cried Wolf. *Pity,*

the word we all dread. Keep them
heebie-jeebies away from my door,
the *mezuzah,* the spare-this-one, says.

Navigable Sorrow

And the days churned by,
navigable sorrow.
—Robert Hass

That March was icy as Grandma's good looks.
We chanced it. Star thistles float. We made a raft,
bet the odds: set our course by Grandpa Henry's

sweet voice. He knew his way around a polka,
led her quite a dance. Can't hardly call them

lovers, though they had three glossy sons to shine
through all the gloom that was, and still is,
Illinois. Monee, the most entangled little burg

that ever God spat out upon the dirt, where
they farmed 20, godforsaken acres, 'longside

my godforsaken Uncle Irv. Irv of the Shiver,
Irv of the Stutter. Deadeye Irv spitting
his barb at an 8-year-old who's grown now

and won't drive across Sacramento to see
if he's shivering still. I navigate by feel

and by the stars. Oh, Little Dipper, Little
Tipsy Bear, my Grandpa could make you
light on all four feet. Polka me round again,

Henry. Just cattails to catch at our ankles.
Our hot breath as sweet as wild oats.

July in Monee, Illinois

Cornstalks that rustled every night, all night.
Horseshoes' *chink-clank* split the yard.
My redheaded Grandpa sweating and crowing,
"A ringer! A ringer, by God!" *Smash!*
The schnapps bottle left Grandma's hand.
"To the trash for the trash," she would say
as her eyes raked his lean, joyous body
in the overalls he seldom changed. Not
for her. She allowed him to touch her
two or three times every year when her blood
bubbled hot, when her ice-blue eyes
softened and threatened to melt. When she
chose to be sorry afterward. When they lay
side by side in their personal sweat
and the puddle between them a well.

One Answer to the Question *Where is Mom?*

Mom lives on Highland Avenue these days
where Dr. Janssen still makes long house calls,
where little Mary Dee is quarantined
with scarlet fever—no one in or out.

Mom lives with sweet-tongued Norm whose tender praise
still tickles her long spine (hushed, conjugal
and secret from his Ma, cold, sneering, mean
to interloping wives who dared to flout

"God's will," Missouri-Synod-Lutheran ways.)
But tipsy Pa slips in to save them all,
wolf-whistling Ma as she bends down to clean
the violets, the cobwebs, crumbs, the doubts.

A Tableau of the Forbidden

Dr. Freud knew the names of the monkeys.
He knew their grandfathers' names.
They were not vagabonds. They owned
real property, right here in Vienna,
staked claims on the pleasant street
next to the Opera House,
on the *strasse* he strolled every night
to get home to his wife and his sister-in-law. Ah,

they all tipped their three-cornered
hats. In their simian noggins,
a waltz played. You could see it
in each gliding step: the Waltz
of the Viennese Gossips
in their silk and lace,
their fancy dress.

The doctor peered over his shoulder.
How they chattered. How wildly they waved.
Was it money these knaves were after?
He flung coins. He emptied his purse. They
broke ranks. They all stuffed their pockets.
They scampered, their ragged parade
shook the *strasse*. The linden trees shuddered
like his sister-in-law in his arms.

God's Messengers

When they come, let them carry me,
feet first and shining, into that radiant room
where the bodies of angels indulge me
with their iridescent white beams.

When they come, let their hands loft me
over their halos. Let me rise like Elijah's
white breath soaring over the stratosphere
into the aether, neon for *What a Good Death*.

When they come, let contraltos and meadowlarks,
let tenors and nightingales praise. Let them
harmonize from the beginning. And let
sunflowers tenderly rise. Let them

bloom out of season, as I did. Let my voice
ring out in your blood, toll and angelus,
echo and blessing: when they come,
when they come, when they come.

The High Lonesome

The high lonesome: those high bluegrass voices in harmony
that will, says Ricky Skaggs, "break your heart, pull your gut out."

When the high lonesome's wailed,
I'm the root of the chord. Brace my feet,
batten my alto down, tune myself to the last,

lonesome cowboy whose guitar
and grandmama's bourbon
can't keep him

from howlin' at stars. The moon
lights him up like a Sunday-school woman,
just a half inch off the rails, like young Maude

handed down off the surrey directly
into the plot. To a man of few words,
and those whispered, as she

took the plunge,
Sunday be damned.

Light in the Corner Where No One Can Find It

Still, what a gift from the gods:
from its shadows, my brother steps
smiling, cocking his gray, crew-cut head.

In a pair of brand-new Converse All Stars,
he has righted himself and he glides.
Keeps the basketball moving

under his right hand,
leaps lightly straight back
into high school. Alights in exactly

the place where the corner
was turned and he
pivots

and 40 years crumble to dust.

The light of day along your face,

its celebrated crevices and crannies.
Whole decades tangled in your fists.
That grip regretting nothing.

First light of day, first day of spring,
you're 81 and "gone." O Norm
of Homewood, Illinois, of feet wet

with mirage. O Norm of speed,
of Cadillac, of moving violation.
O ashes made of Norman

laid down in that double plot,
by some of us. By Mother in
her pink and glowing coat,

her cloud of white hair
and its dark streak
shining.

Documentation

To document: To support (an assertion or a claim, for example) with evidence or decisive information. [from Middle English, precept, instruction, from Old French, from Latin *documentum*: lesson, example, warning]
—*The American Heritage Dictionary of the English Language*

from *A Triptych of Photographs* at the Holocaust Museum

It was documentation: the clothed photograph
as he stood for them, balanced and still. His body

was twisted: a dwarf and malformed, in his
high, polished boots and his gabardine trousers,
in his perfectly pressed linen shirt. Next, they

stripped him down. Thick fingers, calipers, probe,
cameras, dozens of eyes. First, his sloped neck,

the hunch of his shoulders. Next, that roller coaster:
his spine. But his foreshortened legs were a special
delight for the man with the first flashing knife.

And the dwarf knew: his last hour breathing
as the blows fell, yes: blade after blade: 60 blows,

70, 80. And they butchered him then, after death.
Carved the flesh off the armature and washed it clean.
Reassembled it in the same pose: dressed dwarf

and naked dwarf, dwarf's skeleton
making the sequence complete.

In this nightmare,

my sisters are corpses. And since I
must have someone to tell, I dream up
two more, redheads, strangers
so I can watch them recoil.

In bleak Technicolor,
I make me pay. Mea culpa,
my own heart attacks. Rocks
my rib cage. I shudder. I

gasp awake, icy hands
squeezing my chest.
All right: these dreams
came to find me

after I found Uncle Irv
on his bed, fully dressed,
with his face turning black
and the smell of him filling the house.

October Light

1

This afternoon, a valley
parenthesis
of light.

Exact, hard likenesses:
each curl
each ragged, dying leaf.

2

One day in girlhood-Illinois
I raked the whole side yard
with Frankie, Frank Cresenzi.
We outcasts of 6th grade,

in car coats, in red mittens,
wrapped up in fleecy scarves,
we raked and mounded
elm leaves,
a dozen chest-high piles.

Then he, his dark hair curling
above his bright-red ears,
sat down hard on the last mound
and pulled me in his lap.

His arm squeezed tight around my waist.
The leaves
were dry and warm.

We watched the sky
lose color
that whole, long afternoon.

Oh, the Love God he juggle me

roughly. Toss me high
in his big, meaty palms
with the man next door

(flashing his hazel eyes:
22-second lightning strike),
with quotidian men, shining

women (Queen Latifah
in taut, gold lamé). And up
from nowhere, my very first

love with his rosy mouth,
with his golden-brown
tousled curls, my

kindergarten beau:
Billy Burdette. I
was a lummox

at 5. A chunk of a girl,
tallest kid in the class,
a clumsy Illinois

Valkyrie longing
for someone to save. So
when Billy's tears threatened

his dimples as he let
his story fall (how every
sad noon as he

sprinted for home, three
8-year-old bullies
would burst through

the lilac hedge,
jeering and flexing
their fists), I

grand protectress,
just took his hand
and walked

his dainty self home. No,
being a girl didn't save me.
And sweet Billy? Why,

that boy ran. And when it was over,
I righted myself and stumbled
down those shady streets,

tear-streaked and dirty
and smiling in my torn,
blue-and-white gingham dress.

Just an old broken nightmare

you kicked in a corner, keeping
its hands to itself. Still,

I recognized something
desperate about it:

flapping its terrible mouth.

Clara Schumann's last winter as Wife,

she is a vessel, all nipple and cradle.
The seventh child rocks in her womb while
night after long night, the other six
fight sleep and Robert's moans
pierce every dream. Endlessly,
and in both his ears this time:
Concert A summoning, tolling.
That single, implacable note.

Tonight, Schubert and Mendelssohn
blaze through his veins, demanding to be
written down. He clings to her fingers
like any man drowning. While Brahms,
with those sheep's eyes, *dear Clara
Schumann,* beseeches her
with cradle songs.

The Blood-Is-Thicker-Than-Vodka Brother

Some blame the thank-God-it's-Saturday
shindigs where the grownups sipped
martinis, Manhattans, scotch.

Where the kids made the rounds
of the near-empty glasses, danced
the small-body-hits-me-quick reel.

The women said men
went *on sprees,* got *polluted*
on *the booze* or *the sauce*

or *the hooch.* Some *(rummies,*
thirsty souls) just couldn't
stop. Those *pint-in-pocket,*

hair-of-dog drunks just like
the brother who spilled his own
secret, danced the *swillbelly*

two-step, the *old blotto*
shuffle, the *drunk-as-a-lord*
hits-the-ground.

Day after Her Mother Was Killed in the Hit-And-Run, Mary Mae, 14, Readied the Ironing Board

Mary Mae creaked the ironing board open.
Midnight. The kitchen. They slept. She
eased the door closed, lit another lamp
and laid out, on the board's steady surface,
her mother's best blue linen dress.

Mary Mae filled her round cheeks with water,
pursed her lips, sprayed a fine, even arc.
She moistened the cloth, loosed
the wrinkles. The threads
of the blue dress

relaxed. She lifted the flatiron
off the back burner. She spat once
on its pressing plate, testing. Then,
took the iron to the dress. Mary Mae
shaped the square neck, the bodice,

traced the darts that indented the waist.
She eased the iron's tip through the buttons,
pearl ovals that gleamed up the back.
Mary Mae pressed the three-quarter-length sleeves,
made the pleats of the skirt

fall just so. Steam rose:
a halo to bless her
smoothing perfect
that royal-blue linen
in no way resembling a shroud.

My mother's old-fashioned,

steel-gray pressure cooker,
20 years older than God, exploded,
erupted its long-handled lid

on a geyser called Old Not-So-
Faithful, an Etna of beef in its stew
blasting that lid, *thud-punch,*

into the ceiling. She raced it, assessing
trajectory, then dropped, her back
arched like a cat's

to receive its descent, take the weight,
take the brunt like the lace-aproned
soldier she was.

Henry and Anna and Love

For red hair and the polka,
good teeth and strong legs
and the money the whole town
thought his family had,
she married him. August 1913.

There was someone she wanted,
someone poor and timid.
A blond man whose least smile
could make her smile tremble.

Henry, her father said. You'll
marry Henry.

And Henry was easy
to pull here, push there
to manage, to keep
in his place in the bedroom
night after night,
on the floor, on a pallet
guarding her, guarding the door.

He wanted to love that secretive body:
pink glimpses
of nipple, of loose
swaying hip,
pale thighs that opened
like old, rusted scissors.

He could dance Anna breathless,
ribs tapping her corset,
could polka her,
rosy and panting and soft.

It was after a dance
he broke all his promises
under the Star of Hope quilt.

**

Twice more he broke through
those desperate promises:
May 1916, June 1919.
Three times, three sons, three
tangible scars,
three nights he carried
somewhere in his body,
countercharms, memories, dreams

as he slept on his pallet
alone in the hallway, guarding
his family, letting
her rest.

Mornings, she'd pad by.
He'd watch her thin ankles
whisk down the hall
just out of his reach.

But that April morning,
the rooster just crowing,
the windows wide open
to lilac, to lavender

she must have been
sleepwalking, walking so close
the hem of her nightgown
slid over his face. Soft

yellow cotton, thin,
clinging, warm, tore
as he grabbed her, as she tried

to run. As she fell
beside him, it slid
away, open.

So many long nights.
His sons pulled him off.

How They Hear Us All Coming

The click of the bones in Aunt's shoulder,
the moan down the length of her spine
and the whistle that rises up in her throat
from the couch where she flung herself

down. She is trying to dream her way
out of here. She is almost awake. *O! Ramon!*
she cries out as she struggles against it. She is
almost awake. Won't be long.

*

Uncle *chink-chinks* the pennies
in both of his pockets, his belt buckle
steadily chimes. And the slaps of his slippers
keep coming: bedroom, hall, kitchen, backyard.
And his busy head's buzzing its own hive,
the bee stings of fat, errant words
slipping off the loose tongues
of the weary and mean
as they disappear and disappoint.

*

Nephew climbs the walls, slaps at
the windows. That *huff huff*
his desperate breath. His eyes bug.
He is seized, rattled, spine-shook.
His Mama's voice glows in the dark.

They can track her sigh all through
the county. They can find her
'most anywhere now.

If: *blood is thicker than water,*

then consanguinity reigns. But:
there was bad blood between us.
Ask this black sheep

what that means. We decided
to glaze all the old sins
with rainwater after

the last uncle died. For the sake
of the storm that we buried
him in, for the island

he'd made of his pride. We're his
legacy, his brother's children:
four daughters, the only son,

on the road from 10,000 directions
to a place none of us
would call home.

From the raggedy edges I'm mending,

I gather the loose, hungry threads.
They were scarlet and golden and gleaming
when I lifted them off his doorknob. It's the scarf
of my dead uncle, Irvin, with its thin red-and-yellow
wool plaid. What I took from that tumbledown

haven, where an old hermit piled up
his duds. Once upon a time, blue-eyed
and handsome, he crouched in the snow
by my sled for the sake of the family
album, for a dimpled and giggling child.

Bilateral Equation

1

If: levity lifts up my shoulders and gravity
settles my hips, the forces are equal
and balance. The mirror,
trajectory, fits. As: the wings

I imagine on my back mirror the arcs
of old grief. And my spine
takes the brunt, that old willow.
Like a buoy in a storm, how I rock.

2

Levity, gravity's obverse.
Earthworms will tunnel and steal

Uncle Franz, Cousin Petunia,
Dear Dennis, Madame Gorbachev.

Gravitas, solemn and Latin,
taking on substance and weight.

Icarus, melting, defiant. My
shoulder blades twitching yet.

3

The wings I've painted on my back
unfold beneath my skin. Just

this once, Mother, take my hand,
just this time, in this dream:

a *Wanderjahr*: west Africa.
The scenic route: Delphi, Lyon.

That's how I missed the kiss you blew
up Highway 99.

Notes

Meanings of Words in Languages Other Than English

Dorogaya, Russian: dear.

Mezuzah, Yiddish: a tiny oblong container holding verses from Deuteronomy and affixed to the front doorjamb. It consecrates the home.

Pekl, Yiddish: a bundle, a little package. The expression "He always carries his *pekl* with him" is a way of describing a hunchback.

Shiksa, Yiddish: a non-Jewish woman.

Tsuris, Yiddish: troubles, woes.

Vey iz mir, Yiddish: "Woe is me" *or* "It hurts me."

Yarmulke, Yiddish: the skullcap worn by observing Jewish males.

Yortzeit, Yiddish: the anniversary of someone's death.

Other Annotations

The words "God" and "Lord" (used for the Hebrew *Adonai*) are often written by many Jews as "G-d" and "L-rd" as a way of avoiding writing a name of God, so as to avoid the risk of sinning by erasing or defacing His name. In Deuteronomy 12:3–4, the Torah exhorts one to destroy idolatry, adding, "You shall not do such to the LORD your God." From this verse it is understood that one should not erase the name of God. The general rabbinic opinion is that this verse applies only to the sacred Hebrew names of God—but not to the word "God" in English or any other language. Even among Jews who consider it unnecessary, many nonetheless write the name "God" in this way to show respect and to avoid erasing God's name even in a nonforbidden way.

Regarding the poem "Gravity": Greek oral tradition tells us that the young Sophocles sang in the victory choir for the sea battle at Samothrace.

Mary Zeppa's poems have appeared in a variety of print and online journals, including *Perihelion, Switched-on Gutenberg, Zone 3, New York Quarterly,* and *Permafrost,* and in several anthologies, most recently *Beyond Forgetting: Poetry and Prose about Alzheimer's Disease* (Kent State University Press, 2009). Zeppa is the author of two chapbooks, *Little Ship of Blessing* (Poets Corner Press) and *The Battered Bride Overture* (Rattlesnake Press). Zeppa, a founding editor of the *Tule Review,* is also a literary journalist; her interview "Charles Wright on Eugenio Montale and Dino Campana" (*Poet News,* 1985) appears in the 2008 McFarland collection *Charles Wright in Conversation.* She served as executive editor of *Keepers of the Flame: The First Thirty Years of the Sacramento Poetry Center* (Rattlesnake Press, 2009) and currently cohosts the Center's Third Thursdays at the Central Library series. Zeppa is a three-time Resident Fellow at the Virginia Center for the Creative Arts and a 20-year veteran of the a cappella quintet Cherry Fizz.

CPSIA information can be obtained at www.ICGtesting.com
Printed in the USA
BVOW05s1301030315

389742BV00002B/3/P

9 781625 491268